Microsoft
Windows XP
Brief Concepts and Techniques

Gary B. Shelly
Thomas J. Cashman
Steven G. Forsythe

THOMSON
COURSE TECHNOLOGY

COURSE TECHNOLOGY
25 THOMSON PLACE
BOSTON MA 02210

SHELLY
CASHMAN
SERIES.

Australia • Canada • Denmark • Japan • Mexico • New Zealand • Philippines • Puerto Rico • Singapore
South Africa • Spain • United Kingdom • United States

THOMSON
—— ★ ——™
COURSE TECHNOLOGY

Asia (excluding Japan)
Thomson Learning
5 Shenton Way #01-01
UIC Building
Singapore 068808

Japan
Thomson Learning
Nihonjisyo Brooks Bldg 3-F
1-4-1 Kudankita
Chiyoda-Ku
Tokyo 102-0073 Japan

Australia/New Zealand
Nelson/Thomson Learning
102 Dodds Street
South Melbourne, Victoria 3205
Australia

Latin America
Thomson Learning
Seneca, 53
Colonia Polanco
11560 Mexico D.F. Mexico

South Africa
Thomson Learning
Zonnebloem Building,
Constantia Square
526 Sixteenth Road
P.O. Box 2459
Halfway House, 1685
South Africa

Canada
Nelson/Thomson Learning
1120 Birchmount Road
Scarborough, Ontario
Canada M1K 5G4

UK/Europe/Middle East
Thomson Learning
Berkshire House
168-173 High Holborn
London, WC1V 7AA United Kingdom

Spain
Thomson Learning
Calle Magallanes, 25
28015-MADRID
ESPANA

PHOTO CREDITS: *Project 1, pages WIN 1.04-05* Bill Gates, Courtesy of Microsoft Corporation; *Project 2, pages WIN 2.02-03* sports car, sunset, and road, Courtesy of Art Today; computer, Courtesy of PhotoDisc, Inc.; moon landing, Courtesy of Nova Development; other images, Courtesy of Art Today.

ISBN 0-7895-6419-X

5 6 7 8 9 10   BC   06 05 04 03 02

Microsoft

Windows XP

Brief Concepts and Techniques

Contents

Preface

The Shelly Cashman Series® offers the finest textbooks in computer education. We are proud of the fact that our *Microsoft Windows 3.1*, *Microsoft Windows 95*, *Microsoft Windows 98*, and *Microsoft Windows 2000* textbooks have been so well received by instructors and students. The *Windows XP* books continue with the innovation, quality, and reliability found in these previous editions.

In our *Microsoft Windows XP* books, you will find an educationally sound and easy-to-follow pedagogy that combines a step-by-step approach with corresponding screens. The Other Ways and More About features offer in-depth knowledge of Windows XP. The project openers provide a fascinating perspective on the subject covered in the project. The Shelly Cashman Series *Microsoft Windows XP* textbooks will make your computer applications class exciting and dynamic and one that your students will remember as one of their better educational experiences.

Features of Microsoft Windows XP

Microsoft Windows XP is the most significant upgrade since the introduction of Windows 95. The enhancements to Windows XP include: (1) a new look and feel to the user interface; (2) increased reliability and security; (3) increased performance to run programs faster; (4) the ability to create multiple user accounts and easily switch between accounts: (5) a redesigned Start menu and Control Panel; (6) a more comprehensive Help and Support system; (7) increased emphasis on the use of digital media; (8) an easy-to-install home or small office network; and (9) new versions of Windows Media Player, Movie Maker, Internet Explorer, and Windows Messenger.

You can upgrade from your current Windows operating system to either Windows XP Professional or Windows XP Home Edition. Windows XP Professional includes all the features of Windows XP Home Edition, plus extra features for business and power users. For more information about the new features of Windows XP and the differences between Windows XP Professional and Windows XP Home Edition, see Appendix A.

Windows XP and the Figures in This Book

The figures in this book were created using Windows XP Professional. If you plan to step through the projects in this book, you may notice subtle differences between the images on your desktop and the corresponding figure in the book. These differences may be due to the Windows version from which you upgraded; the Internet connection used; or the version of Windows XP installed on the computer. For example, the commands on the Start menu in Home Edition may be different from those in Professional; a button or tab in a dialog box may be different; or a default setting may be different. Although the vast majority of the steps in this book work with both Home Edition and Professional, any steps that do not work with Home Edition are identified.

Objectives of This Textbook

Microsoft Windows XP: Brief Concepts and Techniques is intended for use in a six- to ten-contact-hour course that covers an introduction to Microsoft Windows XP, or in combination with other books in an introduction to computers or computer applications course. No computer experience is assumed. The objectives of this book are:

- To teach the fundamentals and skills necessary to adequately use Windows XP
- To provide a knowledge base for Windows XP upon which students can build

- To expose students to real-world examples and procedures that will prepare them to be skilled users of Windows XP
- To encourage independent study and help those who are working alone in a distance education environment

When students complete the course using this textbook, they will have a basic knowledge and understanding of Windows XP.

The Shelly Cashman Approach

Features of the Shelly Cashman Series *Microsoft Windows XP* books include:

- **Project Orientation:** Related topics are presented using a project orientation that establishes a strong foundation on which students can confidently learn more advanced topics.
- **Screen-by-Screen, Step-by-Step Instructions:** Each task required to complete a project is identified throughout the development of the project. Then, steps to accomplish the task are specified and are accompanied by screens.
- **Thoroughly Tested Projects:** Every screen in the textbook is correct because it is produced by the author only after performing a step, which results in unprecedented quality.
- **Two-Page Project Openers:** Each project begins with a two-page opener that sets the tone for the project by describing an interesting aspect of Windows XP.
- **Other Ways Boxes for Reference:** Microsoft Windows XP provides a variety of ways to carry out a given task. The Other Ways boxes displayed at the end of most of the step-by-step sequences specify the other ways to do the task completed in the steps. Thus, the steps and the Other Ways box make a comprehensive reference unit.
- **More About Feature:** These marginal annotations provide background information about the topics covered, adding interest and depth to learning.

Organization of This Textbook

Microsoft Windows XP: Brief Concepts and Techniques provides instruction on how to use Windows XP. The material is divided into two projects and an appendix:

Project 1 – Fundamentals of Using Microsoft Windows XP In Project 1, students learn about user interfaces and Microsoft Windows XP. Topics include launching Microsoft Windows XP; logging on to the computer; using the Start menu; adding icons to the desktop; maximizing and minimizing windows; moving, sizing, and scrolling windows; launching an application program; using Windows Help and Support; logging off from the computer; and turning off the computer.

Project 2 – Using Windows XP Explorer In Project 2, students learn to use Windows XP Explorer. Topics include launching Windows XP; displaying files, folders, and drive and folder contents in Explorer; expanding a drive or folder; launching an application from Explorer; and copying, moving, renaming, and deleting files in Explorer.

Appendix A - New Features of Windows XP Professional and Windows XP Home Edition Appendix A at the back of this book provides a listing of the new Windows XP features including a comparison that identifies whether the feature is available in both editions.

End-of-Project Student Activities

A notable strength of the Shelly Cashman Series *Microsoft Windows XP* textbooks is the extensive student activities at the end of each project. Well-structured student activities can make the difference between students merely participating in a class and students retaining the information they learn. These activities include:

- **What You Should Know** A listing of the tasks completed within a project together with the pages where the step-by-step, screen-by-screen explanations appear. This section provides a perfect study review for students.
- **Learn It Online** Each project features a Learn It Online page comprised of ten exercises. These exercises utilize the Web to offer project-related reinforcement activities that will help students gain confidence in their Windows XP abilities. These exercises include True/False, Multiple Choice, Short Answer, Flash Cards, Practice Test, Learning Games, Tips and Tricks, Newsgroup usage, Expanding Your Horizons, and Search Sleuth.
- **Use Help** Users of Windows XP must know how to use Help and Support. This book contains extensive Help activities. These exercises alone distinguish the Shelly Cashman Series from any other set of Windows XP instructional materials.
- **In the Lab** These assignments require students to make use of the knowledge gained in the project to solve problems on a computer.
- **Cases and Places** Unique case studies allow students to apply their knowledge to real-world situations. These case studies provide subjects for research papers based on information gained from a resource such as the Internet.

Shelly Cashman Series Teaching Tools

The two categories of ancillary material that accompany this textbook are Teaching Tools (ISBN 0-7895-6427-0) and Online Content. These ancillaries are available to adopters through your Course Technology representative or by calling one of the following telephone numbers: Colleges and Universities, 1-800-648-7450; High Schools, 1-800-824-5179; Private Career Colleges, 1-800-347-7707; Canada, 1-800-268-2222; Corporations with IT Training Centers, 1-800-648-7450; and Government Agencies, Health-Care Organizations, and Correctional Facilities, 1-800-477-3692.

Teaching Tools

The Teaching Tools for this textbook include both teaching and testing aids. The contents of the Teaching Tools CD-ROM are listed below.

- **Instructor's Manual** The Instructor's Manual is made up of Microsoft Word files that include lecture notes, solutions to laboratory assignments, and a large test bank. The files allow you to modify the lecture notes or generate quizzes and exams from the test bank using your own word processing software. Where appropriate, solutions to laboratory assignments are embedded as icons.

- **Figures in the Book** Illustrations for every screen in the textbook are available. Use this ancillary to create a slide show from the illustrations for lecture or to print transparencies for use in lecture with an overhead projector.
- **ExamView** ExamView is a state-of-the-art test builder that is easy to use. ExamView enables you to create printed tests, Internet tests, and computer (LAN-based) tests very quickly. You can enter your own test questions or use the test bank that accompanies ExamView. The test bank is the same as the one described in the Instructor's Manual section.
- **Course Syllabus** Any instructor who has been assigned a course at the last minute knows how difficult it is to come up with a course syllabus. For this reason, sample syllabi are included that can be customized easily to a course.
- **Project Reinforcement** True/false, multiple-choice, and short-answer questions help students gain confidence.
- **Interactive Labs** Eighteen completely updated, hands-on Interactive Labs that take students from ten to fifteen minutes each to step through help solidify and reinforce mouse and keyboard usage and computer concepts. Student assessment is available.
- **PowerPoint Presentation** This lecture ancillary contains a PowerPoint presentation for each project in the textbook. You also may make these Power Point presentations available to students on a network for project review, or to be printed for distribution.

Online Content

If you use Blackboard or WebCT, the test bank for this textbook is free in a simple, ready-to-use format. Visit the Instructor Resource Center for this textbook at course.com to download the test bank, or contact your local sales representative for details.

Acknowledgments

The Shelly Cashman Series would not be the leading computer education series without the contributions of outstanding publishing professionals. First, and foremost, among them is Becky Herrington, director of production and designer. She is the heart and soul of the Shelly Cashman Series, and it is only through her leadership, dedication, and tireless efforts that superior products are made possible. Under Becky's direction, the following individuals made significant contributions to these books: Doug Cowley, production manager; Ginny Harvey, series specialist and developmental editor; Ken Russo, senior Web and graphic designer; Mike Bodnar, associate production manager; Mark Norton, technical analyst; Siva Gogulapati, interactive media manager; Michelle French, cover designer; Christy Otten, Stephanie Nance, and Lisa Ikari, graphic artists; Jeanne Black, Betty Hopkins, and Kellee LaVars, QuarkXPress compositors; Lyn Markowicz, Nancy Lamm, Kim Kosmatka, Pam Baxter, and Marilyn Martin, copyeditors/proofreaders; Cristina Haley, indexer; and Susan Sebok and Kim Clark, contributing writers.

Finally, we would like to thank Richard Keaveny, associate publisher; Cheryl Ouellette, managing editor; Jim Quasney, series consulting editor; Alexandra Arnold and Erin Runyon, product managers; Marc Ouellette, Web product manager; Katie McAllister, marketing manager; and Reed Cotter and Emilie Perreault, editorial assistants.

Gary B. Shelly
Thomas J. Cashman
Steven G. Forsythe

FIGURE 1

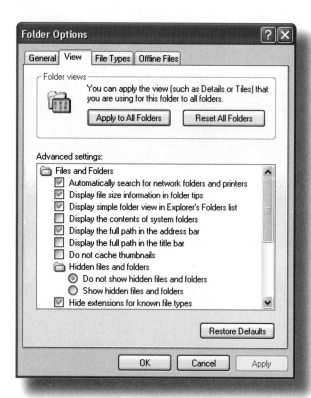

FIGURE 2

Instructions for Restoring the Default Folder Options Settings

The projects and assignments in this textbook are presented using the default folder options settings, as chosen by Microsoft. To ensure your success in completing the projects and assignments, you must install the Windows XP operating system on your computer system and restore the folder options settings. The following steps illustrate how to restore the default folder options settings.

1. Click the Start button and then click the My Computer command on the Start menu.
2. Click Tools on the My Computer menu bar.
3. Click the Folder Options command on the Tools menu to display the Folder Options dialog box (Figure 1).
4. If necessary, click the General tab in the Folder Options dialog box to display the General sheet.
5. On a piece of paper, write down the name of each folder option that is selected in the General sheet in the Folder Options dialog box.
6. Click the Restore Defaults button in the General sheet.
7. Click the View tab to display the View sheet (Figure 2).
8. On a piece of paper, write down the name of each advanced setting that is selected in the View sheet in the Folder Options dialog box.
9. Click the Restore Defaults button in the View sheet.
10. Click the OK button in the Folder Options dialog box.
11. Click the Close button in the My Computer window.

As a result of restoring the default folder option settings, you can perform the steps and assignments in each project of this book. If, after finishing the steps and assignments, you must restore the folder options to their original settings, perform steps 1 through 4 above, click the option button of each setting you wrote down in step 5, perform step 7 above, click the check box and option button of each setting you wrote down in step 8, and then perform step 10 and step 11.

XP

Microsoft

WINDOWS

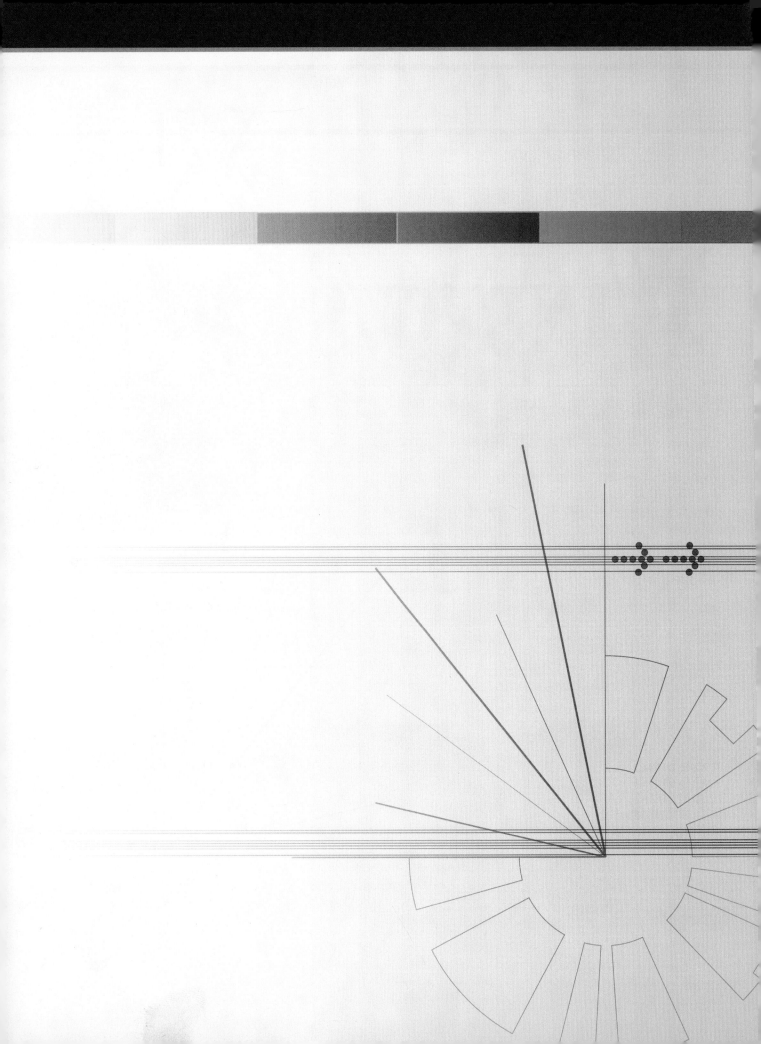

Microsoft Windows XP

Fundamentals of Using Microsoft Windows XP

You will have mastered the material in this project when you can:

O B J E C T I V E S

- Describe Microsoft Windows XP
- Explain operating system, server, workstation, and user interface
- Log on to the computer
- Perform the basic mouse operations: point, click, right-click, double-click, drag, and right-drag
- Identify the objects on the Microsoft Windows XP desktop
- Display the Start menu
- Identify the My Computer and My Documents windows
- Add and remove a desktop icon
- Open, minimize, maximize, restore, and close a Windows XP window
- Move and size a window on the Windows XP desktop
- Scroll in a window
- Understand keyboard shortcut notation
- Launch an application program
- Use Windows XP Help and Support
- Log off from the computer and turn off the computer

Windows XP
Fast at Any Speed

Publicized as the fastest Windows operating system yet, Windows XP continues the momentum with quicker startup, better performance, and a new, simplified visual appearance. Innovative products continue to evolve under the leadership and guidance of Bill Gates, Microsoft's chairman and chief software architect.

Bill Gates's computing efforts began when he was in grade school, when he and classmate, Paul Allen, learned the BASIC programming language from a manual and programmed a mainframe computer using a Teletype terminal they purchased with the proceeds from a rummage sale. In high school, their thirst for more computing power continued. Gates and Allen wrote custom programs for local businesses during the summer and split their $5,000 salaries between cash and computer time. They also debugged software problems at local businesses in return for computer use.

By the time Gates was a sophomore in high school, he was teaching his computer skills to his classmates at the request of one of his teachers. In 1972, Gates and Allen read an article in Electronics magazine about Intel's first microprocessor chip.

They requested a manual from Intel, developed a device that experimented with pushing the chip to its limits, and formed the Traf-O-Data company; an endeavor that ultimately would lead to the formation of something much larger.

In 1973, Gates entered Harvard and Allen landed a programming job with Honeywell. They continued to communicate and scheme about the power of computers.

Then, in 1975, the Altair 8800 computer showed up on the cover of Popular Electronics. This computer was about the size of the Traf-O-Data device and contained a new Intel computer chip. At that point, they knew they were going into business. Gates left Harvard and Allen left Honeywell.

When they formed Microsoft in 1975, the company had three programmers, one product, and revenues of $16,000. The founders had no business plan, no capital, and no financial backing, but they did have a product - a form of the BASIC programming language tailored for the first microcomputer.

IBM approached Microsoft in 1980 and asked the company to provide an operating system for its new IBM personal computer. The deadline? Three months. Gates purchased the core of a suitable

operating system, dubbed Q-DOS (Quick and Dirty Operating System). Microsoft's version, MS-DOS, would become the international standard for IBM and IBM-compatible personal computers. Riding the meteoric rise in sales of IBM-compatible computers and attendant sales of MS-DOS, Microsoft continued to improve its software stream of revisions. At a significant branch of the family tree, Windows made its debut, providing an intuitive graphical user interface (GUI). Similarly, Windows 95, Windows 98, Windows NT, Windows 2000, and Windows Millennium provided further advances.

The Microsoft Windows XP operating system family, Windows XP Professional and Windows XP Home Edition, sets high standards for efficiency and stability and provides advanced productivity and support tools. Appendix A at the back of this book provides a table of new features and compares the two editions. As you complete the projects in this book, you will gain the skills you need to work in the Windows XP environment and see for yourself how its advanced functionality can make your job easier.

Microsoft Windows XP

Fundamentals of Using Microsoft Windows XP

PROJECT 1

C A S E   P E R S P E C T I V E

After weeks of planning, your organization finally installed Microsoft Windows XP on all workstations. As the computer trainer for the upcoming in-house seminar, you realize you should know more about Microsoft Windows XP but have had little time to learn. Since installing Windows XP, many employees have come to you with questions. You have taken the time to answer their questions by sitting down with them at their computers and searching for the answers using the Microsoft Help and Support feature.

From their questions, you determine that you should customize the seminar to cover the basics of Windows XP, including basic mouse operations, working with windows, launching an application, and searching for answers to their questions using Windows XP Help and Support. Your goal is to become familiar with Microsoft Windows XP in order to teach the seminar effectively to the participants.

Introduction

An **operating system** is the set of computer instructions, called a computer program, that controls the allocation of computer hardware such as memory, disk devices, printers, and CD-ROM and DVD drives, and provides the capability for you to communicate with the computer. The most popular and widely used operating system is **Microsoft Windows**. **Microsoft Windows XP**, the newest version of Microsoft Windows, allows you to easily communicate with and control your computer.

Windows XP is easy to use and can be customized to fit individual needs. Windows XP simplifies the processes of working with documents and applications, transferring data between documents, organizing the manner in which you interact with the computer, and using the computer to access information on the Internet or an intranet. The **Internet** is a worldwide group of connected computer networks that allows public access to information on thousands of subjects and gives users the ability to use this information, send messages, and obtain products and services.

Microsoft Windows XP Operating Systems

The Microsoft Windows XP operating systems consist of Microsoft Windows XP Professional and Microsoft Windows XP Home Edition. **Microsoft Windows XP Professional** is the operating system designed for businesses of all sizes and for advanced home computing. In business, Windows XP Professional is commonly used on computer workstations and portable computers. A **workstation** is a computer connected to a server. A **server** is a computer that controls access to the hardware and software on a network and provides a centralized storage area for programs, data, and information. Figure 1-1 illustrates a simple computer network consisting of a server, three computers (called workstations), and a laser printer connected to the server.

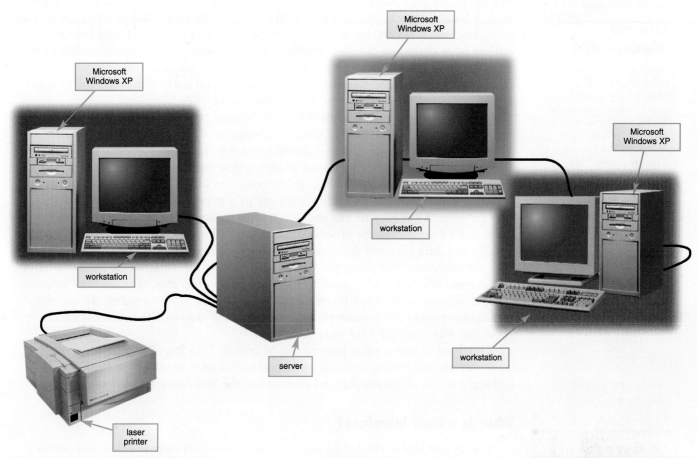

FIGURE 1-1

Microsoft Windows XP Home Edition contains many of the features of the Microsoft Windows XP Professional operating system but is designed for entertainment and home use. Home Edition allows you to establish a network of computers in the home that share a single Internet connection, share a device such as a printer or a scanner, share files and folders, and play multi-computer games. The network can be created using Ethernet cable or telephone wire or can be wireless. For more information about the new features of Windows XP and the differences between Windows XP Professional and Windows XP Home Edition, see Appendix A.

Microsoft Windows XP

Microsoft Windows XP (called **Windows XP** for the rest of the book) is an operating system that performs every function necessary for you to communicate with and use the computer. Windows XP is called a **32-bit operating system** because it uses 32 bits for addressing and other purposes, which means the operating system can address more than four gigabytes of RAM (random-access memory) and perform tasks faster than older operating systems. A **Windows XP 64-Bit Edition** is also available for individuals solving complex scientific problems, developing high-performance design and engineering applications, or creating 3-D animations.

More About

Microsoft Windows XP

Microsoft Windows XP combines the best features of Microsoft Windows 98 with the power and reliability of Microsoft Windows 2000. Windows 98, designed for use on personal computers, is the most popular operating system for personal computers. Windows 2000, designed for use on a computer network, is the most widely used business version of Windows.

Microsoft Windows XP

A vast amount of information about Microsoft Windows XP is available on the Internet. For more information about Microsoft Windows XP, launch the Internet Explorer browser (see pages WIN 1.40 and WIN 1.41), visit the Windows XP More About Web page (scsite.com/winxp/more.htm) and then click All About Microsoft Windows XP.

Windows XP includes several application software programs (Internet Explorer, Windows Media Player, Windows Movie Maker, Windows Messenger, and Outlook Express developed by Microsoft Corporation). **Microsoft Internet Explorer 6** integrates the Windows XP desktop and the Internet. Internet Explorer allows you to work with programs and files in a similar fashion, whether they are located on the computer, a local network, or the Internet. **Windows Media Player 8.0** lets you create and play CDs, watch DVDs, listen to radio stations all over the world, and search for and organize digital media files. **Windows Movie Maker** can transfer recorded audio and video from analog camcorders or digital video cameras to the computer, import existing audio and video files to use in the movies you make, and send the finished movie to a friend by e-mail or post it on the World Wide Web.

Windows Messenger 4.0 is an instant-messaging program that allows you to view who is currently online, send an instant message or a file to a business associate or friend, have a conversation with a group of people, or invite someone to play a game. **Outlook Express 6** is an e-mail program that lets you exchange mail with friends and colleagues, trade ideas and information in a newsgroup, manage multiple mail and news accounts, and add stationery or a personal signature to messages.

Windows XP is easy to use and can be customized to fit individual needs. Windows XP simplifies the process of working with documents and applications by transferring data between documents, organizing the manner in which you interact with the computer, and using the computer to access information on the Internet or an intranet. Windows XP is used to run **application programs**, which are programs that perform an application-related function such as word processing. To use the application programs that can be executed under Windows XP, you must know about the Windows XP user interface.

This book demonstrates how to use Microsoft Windows XP to control the computer and communicate with other computers on a network. In Project 1, you will learn about Windows XP and how to use the Windows XP user interface.

What Is a User Interface?

A **user interface** is the combination of hardware and software that you use to communicate with and control the computer. Through the user interface, you are able to make selections on the computer, request information from the computer, and respond to messages displayed by the computer. Thus, a user interface provides the means for dialogue between you and the computer.

Hardware and software together form the user interface. Among the hardware devices associated with a user interface are the monitor, keyboard, and mouse (Figure 1-2). The **monitor** displays messages and provides information. You respond by entering data in the form of a command or other response using the **keyboard** or **mouse**. Among the responses available to you are responses that specify which application program to run, what document to open, when to print, and where to store data for future use.

The computer software associated with the user interface consists of the programs that engage you in dialogue (Figure 1-2). The computer software determines the messages you receive, the manner in which you should respond, and the actions that occur based on your responses.

The goal of an effective user interface is to be **user-friendly**, which means the software can be used easily by individuals with limited training. Research studies have indicated that the use of graphics can play an important role in aiding users to interact effectively with a computer. A **graphical user interface**, or **GUI** (pronounced gooey), is a user interface that displays graphics in addition to text when it communicates with the user.

The Windows XP Interface

Some older interfaces, called command-line interfaces, required that you type keywords (special words, phrases, or codes the computer understands) or press special keys on the keyboard to communicate with the interface. Today, graphical user interfaces incorporate colorful graphics, use of the mouse, and Web browser-like features, making today's interfaces user-friendly.

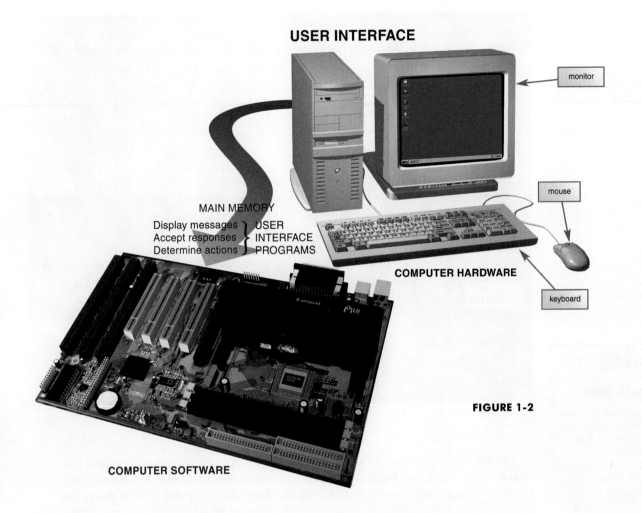

USER INTERFACE

monitor

MAIN MEMORY

Display messages ⎱ USER
Accept responses ⎰ INTERFACE
Determine actions ⎰ PROGRAMS

mouse

COMPUTER HARDWARE

keyboard

COMPUTER SOFTWARE

FIGURE 1-2

The Windows XP graphical user interface was designed carefully to be easier to set up, simpler to learn, faster and more powerful, and better integrated with the Internet than previous versions of Microsoft Windows.

Launching Microsoft Windows XP

When you turn on the computer, an introductory black screen consisting of the Microsoft Windows XP logo, progress bar, copyright messages (Copyright© 1985–2001 and Microsoft Corporation), and the word, Microsoft, displays. The progress bar indicates the progress of launching the Windows XP operating system. After approximately one minute, the Welcome screen displays (Figure 1-3 on the next page).

The **Welcome screen** shows the names of every computer user on the computer. On the left side of the Welcome screen, the Microsoft XP logo and the instructions, To begin, click your user name, display. On the right side of the Welcome screen is a list of the **user icons** and **user names** for all authorized computer users (Annie Meyer, Brad Wilson, and Guest). Clicking the user icon or user name begins the process of logging on to the computer. The list of user icons and names on the Welcome screen on your computer may be different.

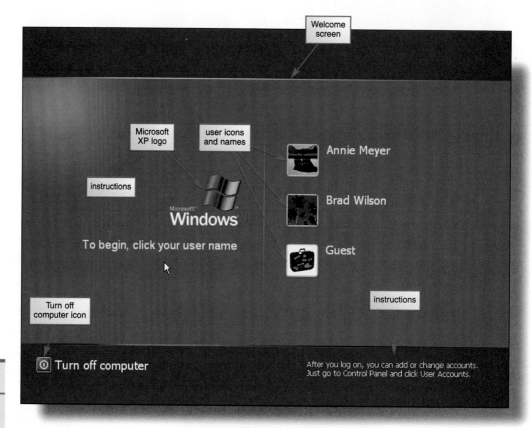

FIGURE 1-3

At the bottom of the Welcome screen is the Turn off computer icon and the instructions, After you log on, you can add or change accounts. Just go to Control Panel and click User Accounts. Clicking the Turn off computer icon initiates the process of shutting down the computer. The **Control Panel** allows you to create a new user, change or remove an existing user, and change user information. The user information that can be changed consists of the user icon and user name, user password, and account type (Administrator, Limited account, and Guest account).

The Windows XP User Interface

The Windows XP user interface provides the means for dialogue between you and the computer. Part of this dialogue involves requesting information from the computer and responding to messages displayed by the computer. You can request information and respond to messages by using either the mouse or the keyboard.

A **mouse** is a pointing device used with Windows XP that is attached to the computer by a cable. Although not required to use Windows XP, Windows XP supports the use of the **Microsoft IntelliMouse** (Figure 1-4). The IntelliMouse contains three buttons, the primary mouse button, the secondary mouse button, and the wheel button between the primary and secondary mouse buttons. Typically, the **primary mouse button** is the left mouse button and the **secondary mouse button** is the right mouse button although Windows XP allows you to switch them. In this book, the left mouse button is the primary mouse button and the right mouse button is the secondary mouse button. The functions the **wheel button** and wheel perform depend on the software application being used. If the mouse connected to the computer is not an IntelliMouse, it will not have a wheel button between the primary and secondary mouse buttons.

Using the mouse, you can perform the following operations: (1) point; (2) click; (3) right-click; (4) double-click; (5) drag; and (6) right-drag. These operations are demonstrated on the following pages.

Many common tasks, such as logging on to the computer, are performed by pointing to an item and then clicking the item. **Point** means you move the mouse across a flat surface until the mouse pointer rests on the item of choice. As you move the mouse across a flat surface, the IntelliEye optical sensor on the underside of the mouse senses the movement of the ball of the mouse (Figure 1-5), and the mouse pointer moves across the desktop in the same direction.

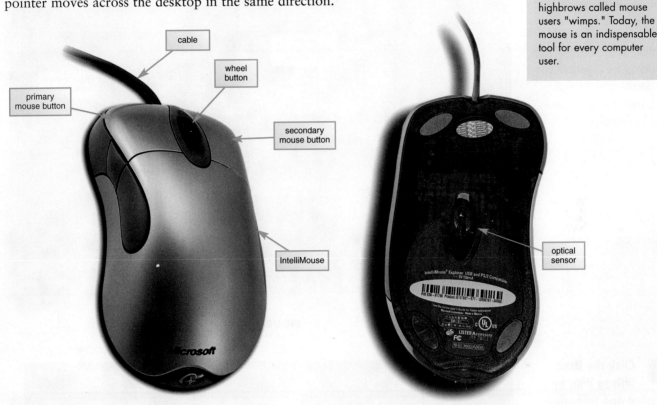

FIGURE 1-4   FIGURE 1-5

Click means you press and release the primary mouse button, which in this book is the left mouse button. In most cases, you must point to an item before you click.

Logging On to the Computer

After launching Windows XP but before working with Windows XP, you must log on to the computer. Logging on to the computer opens your user account and makes the computer available for use. In the steps on the next page, the Brad Wilson icon and the Next button are used to log on to the computer and enter a password. In a school environment, you will want to log on to the computer by pointing to and clicking *your user icon* on the Welcome screen and typing *your password* in the text box instead of the password shown in the steps.

Perform the steps on the next page to log on to the computer by pointing to and clicking your user icon on the Welcome screen, typing your password, and then pointing to and clicking the Next button.

More About

The Mouse

The mouse, though invented in the 1960s, was not used widely until the Apple Macintosh computer became available in 1984. Even then, some highbrows called mouse users "wimps." Today, the mouse is an indispensable tool for every computer user.

More About

Logging on to the Computer

If, after logging on to the computer, you leave the computer unattended for twelve or more minutes, the Welcome screen will display and you will have to log on to the computer again to gain access to your account.

Steps **To Log On to the Computer**

1 **Point to the Brad Wilson icon on the Welcome screen by moving the mouse across a flat surface until the mouse pointer rests on the icon.**

Pointing to the Brad Wilson icon displays a yellow border on the icon and dims the other user icons and names (Figure 1-6).

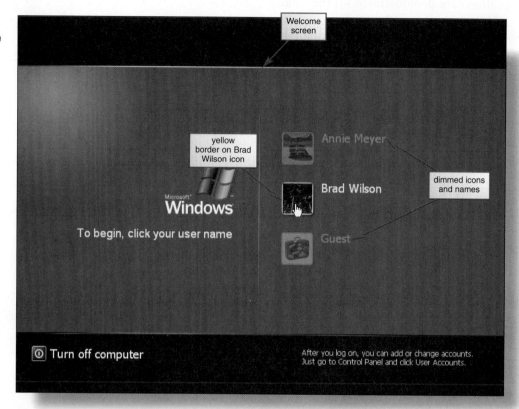

FIGURE 1-6

2 **Click the Brad Wilson icon by pressing and releasing the left mouse button, type** 1akers **in the Type your password text box, and then point to the Next button.**

*Windows XP highlights the Brad Wilson icon and name, displays the Type your password text box containing a series of bullets (••••••) and an insertion point, and the Next and Help buttons (Figure 1-7). A **text box** is a rectangular area in which you can enter text. The bullets in the text box hide the password entered by the user.*

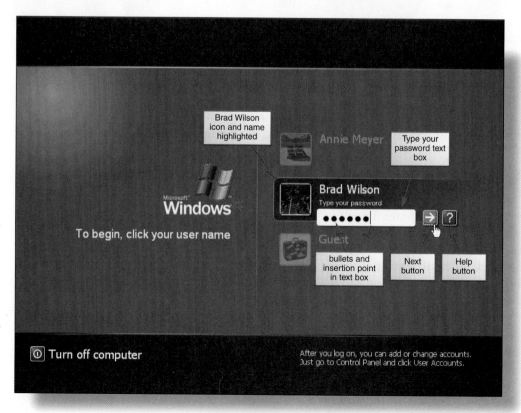

FIGURE 1-7

3 **Click the Next button.**

The contents of the Welcome screen change to contain the word, Welcome, on the left side of the screen and the user name, user icon, and message, Loading your personal settings..., on the right side. This screen displays momentarily while the user is logged on the computer and then several items display on a background called the **desktop** *(Figure 1-8). The background design of the desktop is Bliss, but your computer may display a different design.*

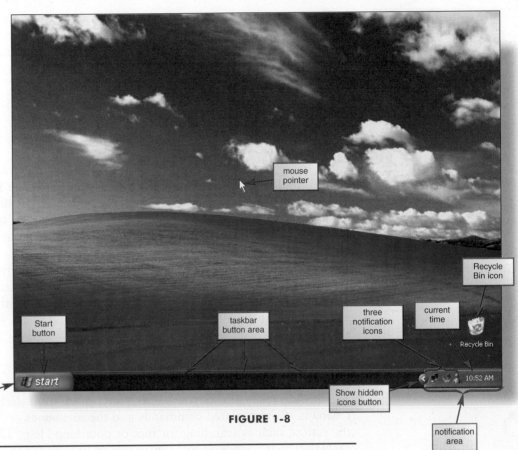

FIGURE 1-8

The items on the desktop in Figure 1-8 include the Recycle Bin icon and its name in the lower-right corner of the desktop and the taskbar at the bottom of the desktop. The Recycle Bin icon (**Recycle Bin**) allows you to discard unneeded objects. Your computer's desktop may contain more, fewer, or different icons because you can customize the desktop of the computer.

The **taskbar** shown at the bottom of the screen in Figure 1-8 contains the Start button, taskbar button area, and notification area. The **Start button** allows you to launch a program quickly, find or open a document, change the computer's settings, obtain Help, shut down the computer, and perform many more tasks. The **taskbar button area** contains buttons to indicate which windows are open on the desktop. In Figure 1-8, no windows display on the desktop and no buttons display in the taskbar button area.

The **notification area** contains the Show hidden icons button, three notification icons, and the current time. The **Show hidden icons button** indicates that one or more inactive icons are hidden from view in the notification area. The three **notification icons** in the notification area provide quick access to programs on the computer. Other icons that provide information about the status of the computer display temporarily in the notification area. For example, the Printer icon displays when a document is sent to the printer and is removed when printing is complete. The notification area on your desktop may contain more, fewer, or different icons because the contents of the notification area can change.

In the center of the desktop is the mouse pointer. On the desktop, the **mouse pointer** is the shape of a block arrow. The mouse pointer allows you to point to objects on the desktop and may change shape when it points to different objects. A shadow may display behind the mouse pointer to make the mouse pointer display in a three-dimensional form.

The Notification Area

The Show hidden icons button displays on the left edge of the notification area if one or more inactive icons are hidden from view in the notification area. Clicking the Show hidden icons button displays the hidden icons in the notification area and replaces the Show hidden icons button with the Hide button. Moving the mouse pointer off the Hide button removes, or hides, the inactive icons in the notification area and redisplays the Show hidden icons button.

When you click an object, such as the Brad Wilson icon or the Next button in Figure 1-7 on page WIN 1.12, you must point to the object before you click. In the steps that follow, the instruction that directs you to point to a particular item and then click is, Click the particular item. For example, Click the Next button means point to the Next button and then click.

The Windows XP Desktop

Nearly every item on the Windows XP desktop is considered an object. Even the desktop itself is an object. Every **object** has properties. The **properties** of an object are unique to that specific object and may affect what can be done to the object or what the object does. For example, a property of an object may be the color of the object, such as the color of the desktop. You will learn more about properties in Project 3 of this book.

The Windows XP desktop and the objects on the desktop emulate a work area in an office. You may think of the Windows desktop as an electronic version of the top of your desk. You can place objects on the desktop, move the objects around on the desktop, look at them and then put them aside, and so on. In Project 1, you will learn how to interact and communicate with the Windows XP desktop.

Displaying the Start Menu

The **Start menu** allows you to easily access the most useful items on the computer. A **menu** is a list of related commands and the **commands** on a menu perform a specific action, such as searching for files or obtaining Help. The Start menu contains commands that allow you to connect to and browse the Internet, launch an e-mail program, launch application programs, store and search for documents, customize the computer, and obtain Help on thousands of topics. Perform the following steps to display the Start menu.

Steps To Display the Start Menu

1 Point to the Start button on the taskbar.

The mouse pointer on the Start button causes the color of the Start button to change to light green and displays a ToolTip (Click here to begin) (Figure 1-9). The ToolTip provides instructions for using the Start button.

FIGURE 1-9

2 Click the Start button.

The Start menu displays (Figure 1-10). The color of the Start button changes to dark green, and the Start button is recessed. The top section of the Start menu contains the user icon and name (Brad Wilson), the middle section contains two columns of commands, and the bottom section contains two commands (Log Off and Turn Off Computer). The commands on the Start menu on your computer may be different.

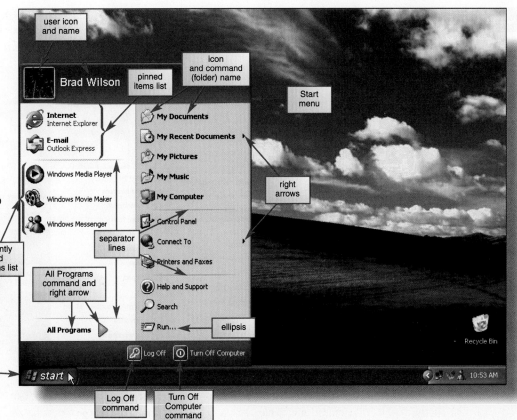

FIGURE 1-10

3 Point to All Programs on the Start menu.

When you point to All Programs, Windows XP highlights the All Programs command on the Start menu by displaying the All Programs command name in white text on a blue background and displays the All Programs submenu (Figure 1-11). A *submenu* is a menu that displays when you point to a command followed by a right arrow. Whenever you point to a command on a menu or submenu, the command name is highlighted.

FIGURE 1-11

4 **Point to Accessories on the All Programs submenu.**

When you point to Accessories, Windows XP highlights the Accessories command on the All Programs submenu and displays the Accessories submenu (Figure 1-12). To launch an application from the Accessories submenu, click the command on the submenu containing the application name. For example, to launch Notepad you would click the Notepad command on the Accessories submenu.

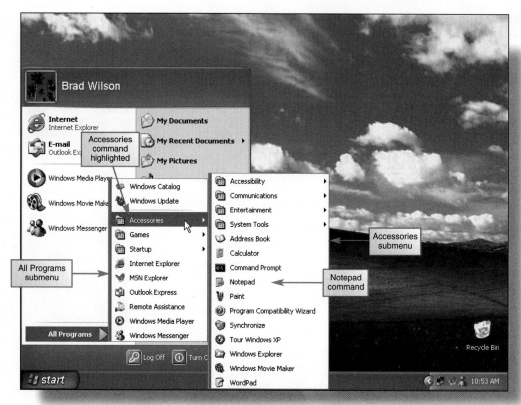

FIGURE 1-12

5 **Point to an open area of the desktop (Figure 1-13).**

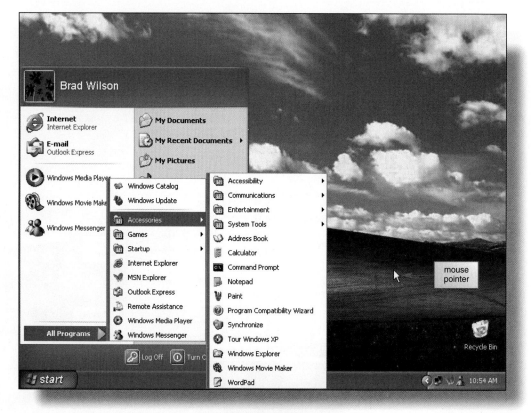

FIGURE 1-13

6 **Click the open area.**

The Start menu, Accessories submenu, and All Programs submenu close, and the recessed dark green Start button changes to its original light green color (Figure 1-14). The mouse pointer points to the desktop. To close any menu, click an open area of the desktop except the menu itself.

Start menu, Accessories submenu, and Programs submenu close

mouse pointer

non-recessed light green Start button

Recycle Bin

start 10:54 AM

FIGURE 1-14

The middle section of the Start menu shown in Figure 1-10 on page WIN 1.15 consists of two columns of commands. Each command is identified by a unique icon and name. Commands may represent an application program, folder, or operation.

The list of commands above the separator line at the top of the left column, called the **pinned items list**, consists of the default Web browser program (Internet Explorer) and default e-mail program (Outlook Express). The list of commands below the separator line, called the **most frequently used programs list**, contains the most frequently used programs. Programs are added to the list when you use them. Currently, three programs (Windows Movie Maker, Windows Media Player, and Windows Messenger) display in the list.

The most frequently used programs list can contain up to six programs. If the list contains less than six programs when you launch a new program, the program name is added to the list. If the list contains six names when you launch a program that is not on the list, Windows XP replaces a less frequently used program with the new program. The All Programs command displays below the separator line at the bottom of the left column.

A list of commands to access various folders displays above the separator line at the top of the right column (My Documents, My Recent Documents, My Pictures, My Music, and My Computer). If the computer is connected to a network, the My Network Places command may display below the My Computer command. Below the separator line are other commands. They are commands to customize the computer (Control Panel), connect to the Internet (Connect To), and add printers and fax printers to the computer (Printers and Faxes). Below the separator line at the bottom of the right column are commands to obtain Help (Help and Support), search for documents and folders (Search), and launch programs (Run).

More About

The Start Menu

The Start menu has finally been redesigned! The Start menu is larger, more colorful, easier to use, and is truly the starting point for using Windows XP. In addition, the Start menu changes to suit the work habits of the user. Commands to access the Internet and an e-mail program, and a constantly changing list of frequently used application commands display prominently on the Start menu. Hooray for innovation!

A **right arrow** following a command in the Start menu indicates that pointing to the command will display a submenu. The All Programs command is followed by a green right arrow and the My Recent Documents and Connect To commands are followed by a smaller black arrow. One command (Run) is followed by an **ellipsis** (...) to indicate more information is required to execute the command.

Windows XP provides a number of ways in which to accomplish a particular task. In the remainder of this book, a single set of steps will illustrate how to accomplish a task. Those steps may not be the only way in which the task can be completed. If you can perform the same task using other means, the Other Ways box specifies the methods. In each case, the method shown in the steps is the preferred method, but it is important for you to be aware of all the techniques you can use.

Adding an Icon to the Desktop

Although the Windows XP desktop may contain only the Recycle Bin icon (see Figure 1-8 on page WIN 1.13), you may want to add additional icons to the desktop. For example, you may want to add the My Computer icon to the desktop so you can view the contents of the computer. One method to view the contents of the computer is to click the My Computer command on the Start menu to open the My Computer window. If you use My Computer frequently, you may want to place the My Computer icon on the desktop where it is easier to find.

One method of adding the My Computer icon to the desktop is to right-click the My Computer command on the Start menu. **Right-click** means you press and release the secondary mouse button, which in this book is the right mouse button. As directed when using the primary mouse button to click an object, normally you will point to the object before you right-click it. Perform the following steps to add the My Computer icon to the desktop.

More About

Desktop Icons

In the past, rows and rows of icons could be seen on Windows desktops. That was the past! Today, the Windows XP desktop contains only the Recycle Bin icon. The Recycle Bin icon, the lone desktop icon, vigilantly waits to dispose of your trash. Yes, the word of the day at Microsoft is uncluttered.

Steps **To Add an Icon to the Desktop**

1 **Click the Start button.**

The Start menu displays and the Start button is recessed (Figure 1-15). The My Computer command displays on the Start menu.

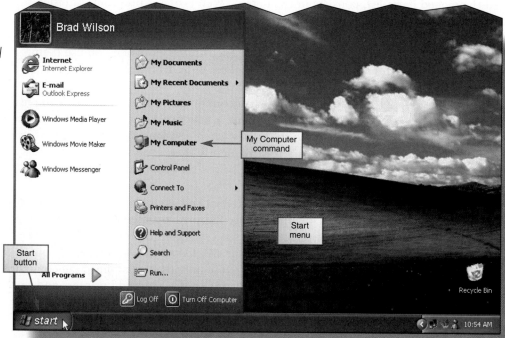

FIGURE 1-15

2   Point to My Computer on the Start menu and then press and release the right mouse button.

*Windows XP highlights the My Computer command and displays a shortcut menu containing nine commands (Figure 1-16). Right-clicking an object, such as the My Computer command, displays a **shortcut menu** that contains commands specifically for use with that object.*

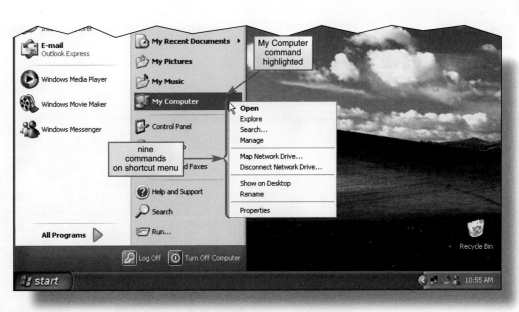

FIGURE 1-16

3   Point to Show on Desktop on the shortcut menu.

When you point to Show on Desktop, Windows XP highlights the Show on Desktop command (Figure 1-17).

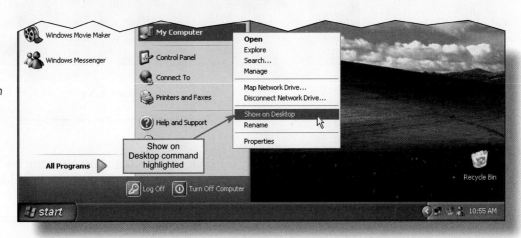

FIGURE 1-17

4   Click Show on Desktop.

The shortcut menu closes and the My Computer icon displays on the desktop (Figure 1-18). The Start menu remains on the desktop.

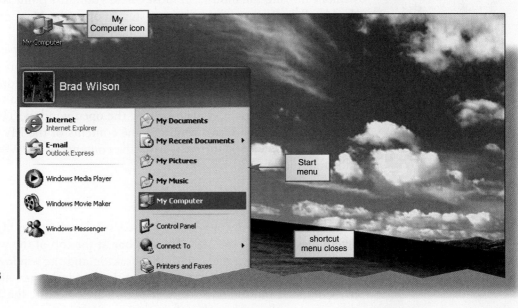

FIGURE 1-18

5 **Click an open area on the desktop to close the Start menu.**

The Start menu closes (Figure 1-19). The My Computer icon and mouse pointer remain on the desktop.

FIGURE 1-19

More About

The Right Mouse Button

The earliest versions of Microsoft Windows made little use of the right mouse button. In Windows XP, the right mouse button makes it easy to display a list of commands for an object (called a shortcut menu) and to copy and move objects on the desktop.

Whenever you right-click an object, a shortcut menu will display. As you will see, the use of shortcut menus speeds up your work and adds flexibility to your interaction with the computer.

Opening a Window Using a Desktop Icon

Double-click means you quickly press and release the left mouse button twice without moving the mouse. In most cases, you must point to an item before you double-click. Perform the following step to open the My Computer window by double-clicking the My Computer icon on the desktop.

In Figure 1-20, the My Computer window, the only open window, is the active window. The **active window** is the window you currently are using or that currently is selected. Whenever you click an object that opens a window, such as the My Computer icon, Windows XP will open the window; and a recessed dark blue button in the taskbar button area will identify the open window. The recessed dark blue button identifies the active window. The contents of the My Computer window on your computer may be different from the contents of the My Computer window shown in Figure 1-20.

The My Computer Window

The thin blue line, or **window border**, surrounding the My Computer window determines its shape and size. The **title bar** at the top of the window contains a small icon that is similar to the icon on the desktop and the **window title** (My Computer) identifies the window. The color of the title bar (dark blue) and the recessed dark blue My Computer button in the taskbar button area indicate the My Computer window is the active window. The color of the active window on your computer may be different.

Steps **To Open a Window Using a Desktop Icon**

1 Point to the My Computer icon on the desktop and then double-click by quickly pressing and releasing the left mouse button twice without moving the mouse.

The My Computer window opens and the recessed dark blue My Computer button displays in the taskbar button area (Figure 1-20). The My Computer window allows you to view the contents of the computer.

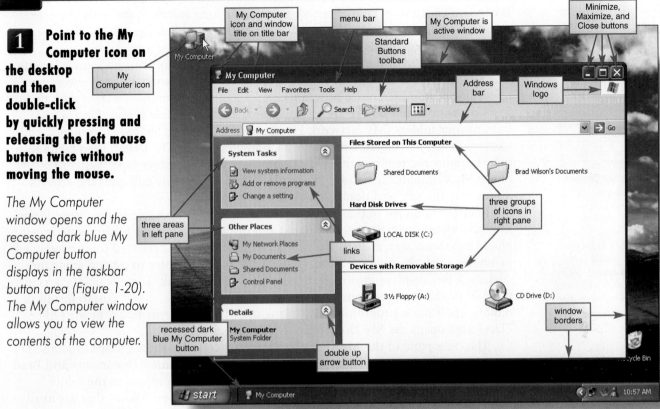

FIGURE 1-20

Clicking the icon at the left on the title bar will display the **System menu**, which contains commands to carry out the actions associated with the My Computer window. At the right on the title bar are three buttons, the Minimize button, the Maximize button, and the Close button, that can be used to specify the size of the window or close the window.

The **menu bar**, which is the horizontal bar below the title bar of a window, contains a list of menu names for the My Computer window: File, Edit, View, Favorites, Tools, and Help. The Windows logo displays on the far right of the menu bar.

The Standard buttons toolbar displays below the menu bar. The **Standard Buttons toolbar** allows you to perform often-used tasks more quickly than using the menu bar. Each button on the Standard Buttons toolbar contains an icon. Three buttons contain a **text label** (Back, Search, and Folders) that identifies the function of the button. Each button will be explained in detail as it is used. The buttons on the Standard Buttons toolbar on your computer may be different.

Below the Standard Buttons toolbar is the Address bar. The **Address bar** allows you to launch an application, display a document, open another window, and search for information on the Internet. The Address bar contains the Address box which includes the My Computer icon, window title, down arrow, and the Go button.

The area below the Address bar is divided into two panes. The System Tasks, Other Places, and Details areas display in the left pane. A title identifies each area. A button displays to the right of the title in each area to indicate whether the area is

Other **Ways**

1. Right-click desktop icon, click Open
2. Press WINDOWS+E (WINDOWS key on Microsoft Natural keyboard)

More **About**

The Contents of the My Computer Window

Because windows are easily customized, your My Computer window may not resemble the window in Figure 1-20. For example, different toolbars may display below the menu bar, icons may display smaller, grouping of icons may not display, and different areas may display in the left pane of the window.

My Computer

While the trade press and media once poked fun at the My Computer name, Microsoft continues to expand the concept. Windows XP now showcases the My Computer, My Documents, My Pictures, and My Music names by placing them on the Start menu. In addition, the new My Videos folder also was added to the operating system. Microsoft contends that beginners find these names easier to understand.

expanded or collapsed. A button identified by a **double up arrow** indicates the area is expanded. A button identified by a **double down arrow** indicates the area is collapsed. When you click the double up arrow button, the area collapses and only the title and the double down arrow button display. When you click the double down arrow button, the area expands and the entire contents of the area are visible.

All three areas in the left pane in Figure 1-20 on the previous page are expanded. The **System Tasks area** contains a title (System Tasks) and three tasks (View system information, Add or remove programs, and Change a setting) associated with the My Computer window. The **Other Places area** contains a title (Other Places) and links to four folders (My Network Places, My Documents, Shared Documents, and Control Panel) associated with the My Computer folder. The **Details area** contains a title (Details), the window title (My Computer), and the folder type (System Folder) of the My Computer window. Clicking the double up arrow collapses the area and leaves only the title and double down arrow button.

Pointing to a task in the System Tasks area or a folder name in the Other Places area underlines the task or folder name and displays the task or folder name in light blue. Underlined text, such as the task and folder names, is referred to as a **hyperlink**, or simply a **link**. Pointing to a link changes the mouse pointer to a hand icon, and clicking a link displays information associated with the link. For example, clicking the Add or remove programs task in the System Tasks area allows you to install or remove application programs and clicking the My Documents folder in the Other Places area opens the My Documents window.

The right pane of the My Computer window contains three groups of icons. The top group, Files Stored on This Computer, contains the Shared Documents and Brad Wilson's Documents icons. A title to the right of each icon identifies the folder names. The **Shared Documents folder** contains documents and folders that are available (shared) to other computer users on the network, and Brad Wilson's Documents contains his personal documents.

The middle group, Hard Disk Drives, contains the LOCAL DISK (C:) drive icon. A title to the right of the icon identifies the drive name, LOCAL DISK (C:). The bottom group, Devices with Removable Storage, contains the 3½ Floppy (A:) and CD Drive (D:) icons and labels. The three icons in the Hard Disk Drives and Devices with Removable Storage sections, called **drive icons**, represent a hard disk drive, 3½ floppy drive, and a Compact Disc drive. The number of groups in the right pane and the icons in the groups on your computer may be different.

Clicking a drive or folder icon selects the icon in the right pane and displays details about the drive or folder in the areas in the left pane. Double-clicking a drive or folder icon allows you to display the contents of the corresponding drive or folder in the right pane and information about the drive or folder in the areas in the left pane. You may find more, fewer, or different drive and folder icons in the My Computer window on your computer.

Minimizing Windows

Windows management on the Windows XP desktop is important in order to keep the desktop uncluttered. You will find yourself frequently minimizing windows and then later reopening them with a click of a button in the taskbar button area.

Minimizing a Window

Two buttons on the title bar of a window, the Minimize button and the Maximize button, allow you to control the way a window displays or does not display on the desktop. When you click the **Minimize button** (Figure 1-20 on the previous page), the My Computer window no longer displays on the desktop and the recessed dark blue My Computer button in the taskbar button area changes to a non-recessed medium blue button. A minimized window still is open but does not display on the screen. To minimize and then redisplay the My Computer window, complete the following steps.

Steps To Minimize and Redisplay a Window

1 **Point to the Minimize button on the title bar of the My Computer window.**

The mouse pointer points to the Minimize button on the My Computer window title bar, the color of the Minimize button changes to light blue, a ToolTip displays below the Minimize button, and the recessed dark blue My Computer button displays on the taskbar (Figure 1-21).

FIGURE 1-21

2 **Click the Minimize button.**

When you minimize the My Computer window, Windows XP removes the My Computer window from the desktop, the My Computer button changes to a non-recessed button, and the color of the button changes to medium blue (Figure 1-22).

FIGURE 1-22

3 **Click the My Computer button in the taskbar button area.**

The My Computer window displays in the same place and size as it was before being minimized and the My Computer button on the taskbar is recessed (Figure 1-23). With the mouse pointer pointing to the My Computer button, the color of the button is medium blue. Moving the mouse pointer off the button changes the color to dark blue. The My Computer window is the active window because it contains the dark blue title bar.

FIGURE 1-23

Other Ways

1. Click icon on left side of title bar, click Minimize, in taskbar button area click taskbar button
2. Right-click title bar, click Minimize, on taskbar button area click taskbar button
3. Press WINDOWS+M (WINDOWS key on Microsoft Natural keyboard), press WINDOWS+SHIFT+M

More About

Maximizing Windows

Many application programs run in a maximized window by default. Often you will find that you want to work with maximized windows to better view the contents of the window. Did you know that double-clicking the title bar also maximizes a window?

Whenever a window is minimized, it does not display on the desktop but a non-recessed dark blue button for the window does display in the taskbar button area. Whenever you want a minimized window to display and be the active window, click its button in the taskbar button area.

As you point to many objects when you work with Windows XP, such as a button or command, Windows XP displays a ToolTip. A **ToolTip** is a short on-screen note associated with the object to which you are pointing. ToolTips display on the desktop for approximately five seconds. Examples of ToolTips are shown in Figure 1-9 on page WIN 1.14, Figure 1-21 on page WIN 1.23, Figure 1-24, and Figures 1-26 and 1-28 on the following pages. To reduce clutter on the screen, the ToolTips will not be shown on the remaining screens in this book.

Maximizing and Restoring a Window

Sometimes when information displays in a window, the information is not completely visible. One method of displaying the entire contents of a window is to enlarge the window using the **Maximize button**. The Maximize button maximizes a window so the window fills the entire screen, making it easier to see the contents of the window. When a window is maximized, the **Restore Down button** replaces the Maximize button on the title bar. Clicking the Restore Down button will return the window to its size before maximizing. To maximize and restore the My Computer window, complete the steps on the next page.

Steps To Maximize and Restore a Window

1 **Point to the Maximize button on the title bar of the My Computer window.**

The mouse pointer points to the Maximize button on the My Computer window title bar and the color of the Maximize button changes to light blue (Figure 1-24). A ToolTip identifying the button name displays below the Maximize button.

FIGURE 1-24

2 **Click the Maximize button.**

The My Computer window expands so it and the taskbar fill the desktop (Figure 1-25). The Restore Down button replaces the Maximize button, the My Computer button in the taskbar button area does not change, and the My Computer window still is the active window.

FIGURE 1-25

3 **Point to the Restore Down button on the title bar of the My Computer window.**

The mouse pointer points to the Restore Down button on the My Computer window title bar and the color of the Restore Down button changes to light blue (Figure 1-26). A ToolTip displays below the Restore Down button identifying it.

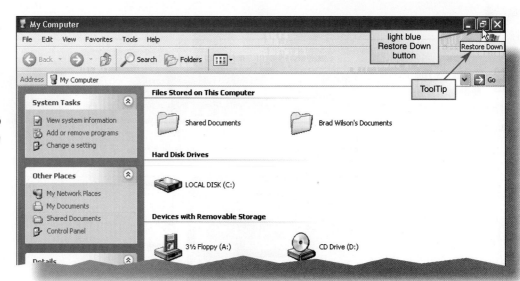

FIGURE 1-26

4 **Click the Restore Down button.**

The My Computer window returns to the size and position it occupied before being maximized (Figure 1-27). The My Computer button does not change. The Maximize button replaces the Restore Down button.

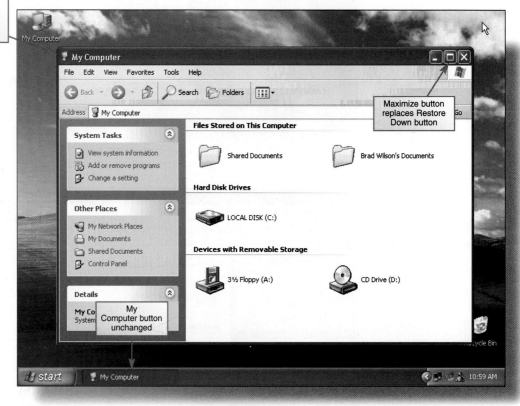

FIGURE 1-27

1. Click icon on left side of title bar, click Maximize, click icon on left of title bar, click Restore
2. Right-click title bar, click Maximize, right-click title bar, click Restore
3. Double-click title bar, double-click title bar

When a window is maximized, such as in Figure 1-25 on the previous page, you also can minimize the window by clicking the Minimize button. If, after minimizing the window, you click its button in the taskbar button area, the window will return to its maximized size.

Closing a Window

The **Close button** on the title bar of a window closes the window and removes the taskbar button from the taskbar. To close and then reopen the My Computer window, complete the following steps.

Steps **To Close a Window**

1 **Point to the Close button on the title bar of the My Computer window.**

The mouse pointer points to the Close button on the My Computer window title bar and the color of the Close button changes to light red (Figure 1-28). A ToolTip displays below the Close button.

FIGURE 1-28

2 **Click the Close button.**

The My Computer window closes and the My Computer button no longer displays in the taskbar button area (Figure 1-29).

Other Ways

1. Click icon on left side of title bar, click Close
2. Right-click title bar, click Close
3. Press ALT+F4

FIGURE 1-29

More *About*

Opening a Window

Although the preferred method of opening a window in previous Windows versions was to double-click a desktop icon, the redesigned Start menu now makes it easier to open those windows.

Opening a Window Using the Start Menu

Previously, you opened the My Computer window by double-clicking the My Computer icon on the desktop. Another method of opening a window and viewing the contents of the window is to click a command on the Start menu. Perform the following steps to open the My Documents window using the My Documents command on the Start menu.

Steps **To Open a Window Using the Start Menu**

1 **Click the Start button on the taskbar and then point to the My Documents command on the Start menu.**

The Start menu displays, the Start button is recessed on the taskbar, the color of the button changes to dark green, and the mouse pointer points to the highlighted My Documents command on the Start menu (Figure 1-30).

FIGURE 1-30

2 **Click My Documents on the Start menu.**

The My Documents window opens, the recessed dark blue My Documents button displays in the taskbar button area, and the My Documents window is the active window (Figure 1-31). You may find more, fewer, or different folder icons in the right pane on your computer.

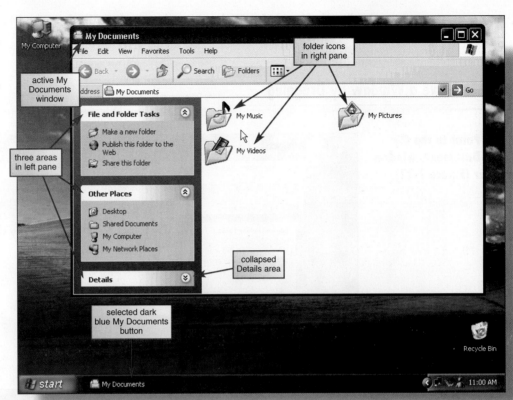

FIGURE 1-31

The My Documents Window

The **My Documents window** shown in Figure 1-31 is a central location for the storage and management of documents. The title bar at the top of the My Documents window identifies the window and the color of the title bar (dark blue) and the recessed dark blue My Documents button in the taskbar button area indicate the My Documents window is the active window.

The File and Folder Tasks, Other Places, and Details areas display in the left pane. The **File and Folder Tasks area** contains three tasks (Make a new folder, Publish this folder to the Web, and Share this folder). The **Other Places area** contains links to four folders (Desktop, Shared Documents, My Computer, and My Network Places). The **Details area** is collapsed and only the title and a double down arrow button display in the area.

The right pane of the My Documents window contains the My Music, My Pictures, and My Videos folders. Clicking a folder icon in the right pane highlights the icon in the right pane and changes the files and folder tasks in the File and Folder Tasks area in the left pane. Double-clicking a folder icon displays the contents of the corresponding folder in the right pane, adds another area to the folder (My Music Tasks area, My Pictures Tasks area, or My Videos Tasks area) in the left pane, and changes the file and folder information in the left pane.

Moving a Window by Dragging

Drag means you point to an item, hold down the left mouse button, move the item to the desired location, and then release the left mouse button. You can move any open window to another location on the desktop by pointing to the title bar of

Other Ways

1. Click Start button, right-click command, click open

More About

Dragging

Dragging is the second-most difficult skill to learn with a mouse. You may want to practice dragging a few times so you will be comfortable with it. Do not let dragging become a drag — PRACTICE!!

the window and then dragging the window. To drag the My Documents window to the center of the desktop, perform the following steps.

Steps **To Move a Window by Dragging**

1 **Point to the My Documents window title bar (Figure 1-32).**

FIGURE 1-32

2 **Hold down the left mouse button, move the mouse down so the window moves to the center of the desktop, and then release the left mouse button.**

As you drag the My Documents window, the window moves across the desktop. When you release the left mouse button, the window displays in its new location on the desktop (Figure 1-33).

FIGURE 1-33

1. Click icon on left side of title bar, click Move, drag window

Expanding an Area

The Details area in the My Documents window is collapsed and a double down arrow button displays to the right of the Details title (Figure 1-34). Clicking the button or the area title expands the Details area and reveals the window title (My Documents) and folder type (System Folder) in the Details area. Similarly, clicking the double up arrow button or the area title collapses the area so only the area title and double down arrow button display in the area. Perform the following steps to expand the Details area in the left pane of the My Documents window.

Steps **To Expand an Area**

1 Point to the double down arrow button in the Details area.

The mouse pointer changes to a hand icon and points to the double down arrow button in the Details area and the color of the Details title and button changes to light blue (Figure 1-34).

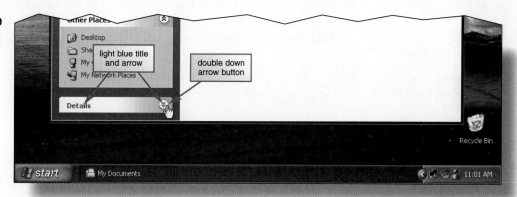

FIGURE 1-34

2 Click the double down arrow button.

The Details area expands, the window title (My Documents) and folder type (System Folder) display in the area, the double down arrow on the button changes to a double up arrow, a portion of the left pane is not visible, and a scroll bar displays in the area (Figure 1-35). If a scroll bar does not display, resize the window to resemble the window in Figure 1-35.

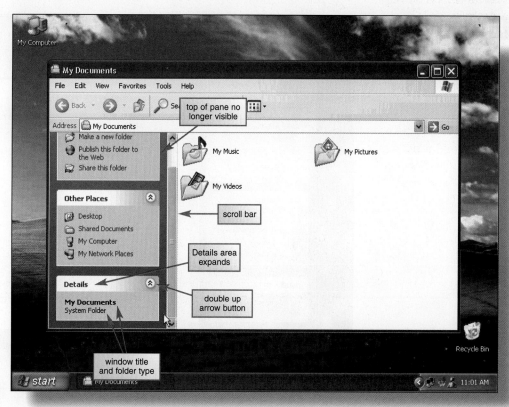

Other Ways

1. Click area title

FIGURE 1-35

Window Sizing

Windows XP remembers the size of the window when you close the window. When you reopen the window, it will display in the same size as when you closed it.

Scrolling

Most people will either maximize a window or size it so all the objects in the window are visible to avoid scrolling because scrolling takes time. It is more efficient not to have to scroll in a window.

A **scroll bar** is a bar that displays when the contents of a pane or window are not completely visible. A vertical scroll bar contains an **up scroll arrow**, a **down scroll arrow**, and a **scroll box** that enable you to view areas that currently are not visible. A vertical scroll bar displays along the right side of the left pane in the My Documents window shown in Figure 1-35 on the previous page. In some cases, the vertical scroll bar also may display along the right side of the right pane in a window.

Scrolling in a Window

Previously, the My Documents window was maximized to display information that was not completely visible in the My Documents window. Another method of viewing information that is not visible in a window is to use the scroll bar.

Scrolling can be accomplished in three ways: (1) click the scroll arrows; (2) click the scroll bar; and (3) drag the scroll box. On the following pages, you will use the scroll bar to scroll the contents of the left pane of the My Documents window.

Perform the following steps to scroll the left pane using the scroll arrows.

 To Scroll Using Scroll Arrows

1 **Point to the up scroll arrow on the vertical scroll bar.**

The color of the up scroll arrow changes to light blue (Figure 1-36).

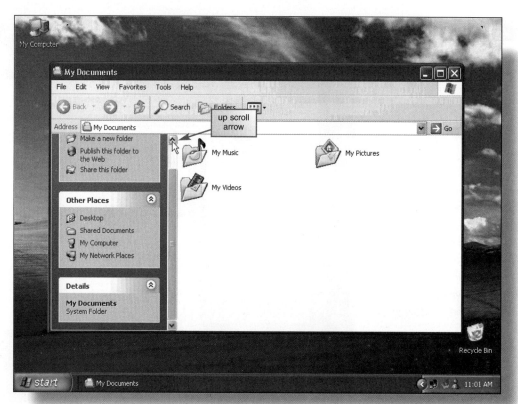

FIGURE 1-36

2 **Click the up scroll arrow two times.**

The left pane scrolls down (the contents in the left pane move up) and displays a portion of the text in the File and Folder Tasks area at the top of the pane that previously was not visible (Figure 1-37). Because the size of the left pane does not change when you scroll, the contents in the left pane will change, as seen in the difference between Figure 1-36 and Figure 1-37.

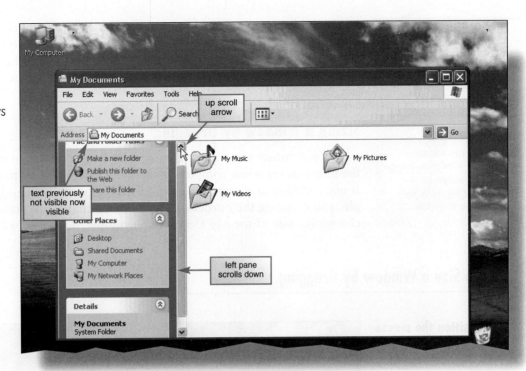

FIGURE 1-37

3 **Click the up scroll arrow three more times.**

The scroll box moves to the top of the scroll bar and the remaining text in the File and Folder Tasks area displays (Figure 1-38).

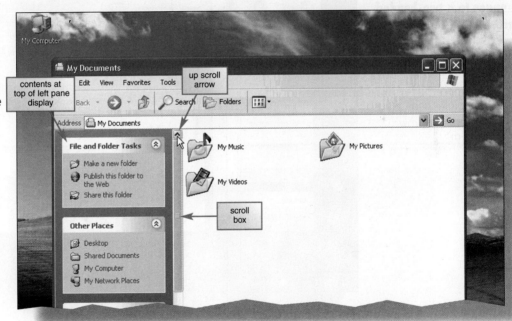

FIGURE 1-38

You can scroll continuously using scroll arrows by pointing to the up or down scroll arrow and holding down the left mouse button. The area being scrolled continues to scroll until you release the left mouse button or you reach the top or bottom of the area. You also can scroll by clicking the scroll bar itself. When you click the scroll bar, the area being scrolled moves up or down a greater distance than when you click the scroll arrows.

The Scroll Bar

In many application programs, clicking the scroll bar will move the window a full screen's worth of information up or down. You can step through a word processing document screen by screen, for example, by clicking the scroll bar.

The third way in which you can scroll is by dragging the scroll box. When you drag the scroll box, the area being scrolled moves up or down as you drag.

Being able to view the contents of a pane or window by scrolling is an important Windows XP skill because in many cases the entire contents of a pane or window are not visible.

Sizing a Window by Dragging

As previously mentioned, sometimes when information displays in a window, the information is not completely visible. A third method to display information that is not visible is to change the size of the window by dragging the window. For example, you can drag the border of a window to change the size of the window. To change the size of the My Documents window, perform the following steps.

Steps To Size a Window by Dragging

1 Position the mouse pointer over the bottom border of the My Documents window until the mouse pointer changes to a two-headed arrow.

When the mouse pointer is on top of the bottom border of the My Documents window, the pointer changes to a two-headed arrow (Figure 1-39).

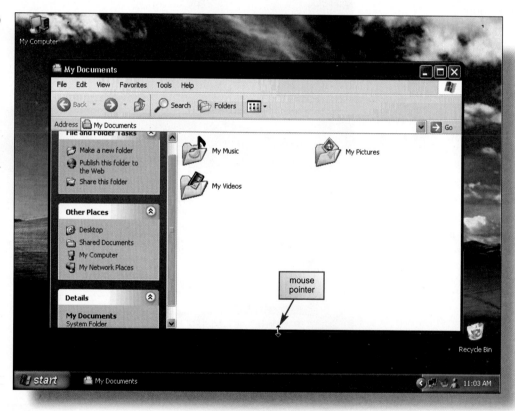

FIGURE 1-39

2 Drag the bottom border downward until the entire Details area is visible in the My Documents window.

As you drag the bottom border, the My Documents window, vertical scroll bar, and scroll box change size. After dragging, the Details area is visible and the vertical scroll bar is no longer visible (Figure 1-40).

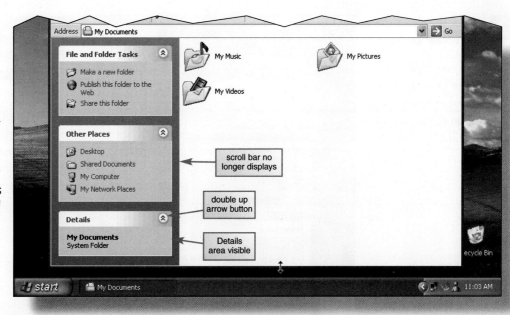

FIGURE 1-40

In addition to dragging the bottom border of a window, you also can drag the other borders (left, right, and top) and any window corner. If you drag a vertical border (left or right), you can move the border left or right. If you drag a horizontal border (top or bottom), you can move the border of the window up or down. If you drag a corner, you can move the corner up, down, left or right.

Collapsing an Area

The Details area in the My Documents window is expanded and a double up arrow button displays to the right of the Details title (Figure 1-40). Clicking the button or the area title collapses the Details area and removes the window title (My Documents) and folder type (System Folder) from the Details area. Perform the following steps to collapse the Details area in the My Documents window.

 To Collapse an Area

1 Point to the double up arrow button in the Details area.

The mouse pointer changes to a hand icon, points to the double up arrow button in the Details area, and the color of the Details title and button changes to light blue (Figure 1-41).

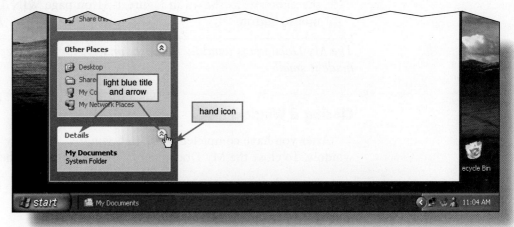

FIGURE 1-41

2 **Click the double up arrow button.**

The Details area collapses and only the Details title and the double down arrow button display (Figure 1-42).

FIGURE 1-42

Other Ways

1. Click area title

Resizing a Window

After moving and resizing a window, you may wish to return the window to approximately its original size. To return the My Documents window to about its original size, complete the following steps.

TO RESIZE A WINDOW

1 Position the mouse pointer over the bottom border of the My Documents window border until the mouse pointer changes to a two-headed arrow.

2 Drag the bottom border of the My Documents window up until the window is the same size as shown in Figure 1-31 on page WIN 1.29 and then release the mouse button.

The My Documents window is approximately the same size as it was before you made it smaller.

Closing a Window

After you have completed work in a window, normally you will close the window. To close the My Documents window, complete the following steps.

TO CLOSE A WINDOW

1 Point to the Close button on the right of the title bar in the My Documents window.

2 Click the Close button.

The My Documents window closes and the desktop contains no open windows.

Deleting a Desktop Icon by Right-Dragging

The My Computer icon remains on the desktop. In many cases after you have placed an icon on the desktop, you will want to delete the icon. Although Windows XP has many ways to delete desktop icons, one method of removing the My Computer icon from the desktop is to right-drag the My Computer icon to the Recycle Bin icon on the desktop. **Right-drag** means you point to an item, hold down the right mouse button, move the item to the desired location, and then release the right mouse button. When you right-drag an object, a shortcut menu displays. The shortcut menu contains commands specifically for use with the object being dragged.

When you delete an icon from the desktop, Windows XP places the item in the **Recycle Bin**, which is an area on the hard disk that contains all the items you have deleted not only from the desktop but also from the hard disk. When the Recycle Bin becomes full, you can empty it. Up until the time you empty the Recycle Bin, you can recover deleted items from the Recycle Bin. To delete the My Computer icon by right-dragging the icon to the Recycle Bin icon, perform the following steps.

More About

Right-Dragging

Right-dragging was not available on some earlier versions of Windows, so you might find people familiar with Windows not even considering right-dragging. Because it always produces a shortcut menu, right-dragging is the safest way to drag.

Steps To Delete a Desktop Icon by Right-Dragging

1 **Point to the My Computer icon on the desktop. Hold down the right mouse button, drag the My Computer icon over the Recycle Bin icon on the desktop, and then release the right mouse button. Point to Move Here on the shortcut menu.**

The My Computer icon displays on the desktop as you drag the icon. When you release the right mouse button, the My Computer icon no longer displays and a shortcut menu displays on the desktop (Figure 1-43). The shortcut menu contains the highlighted Move Here command and the Cancel command.

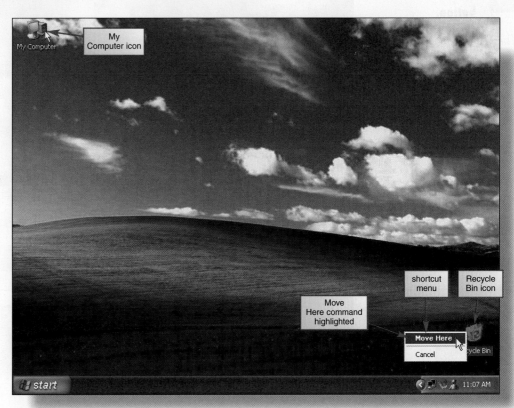

FIGURE 1-43

2 **Click Move Here and then point to the Yes button in the Confirm Delete dialog box.**

*The shortcut menu no longer displays on the desktop and the Confirm Delete dialog box displays on the desktop (Figure 1-44). A **dialog box** displays whenever Windows XP needs to supply information to you or wants you to enter information or select among several options. The Confirm Delete dialog box contains a question, a message, and the Yes and No buttons.*

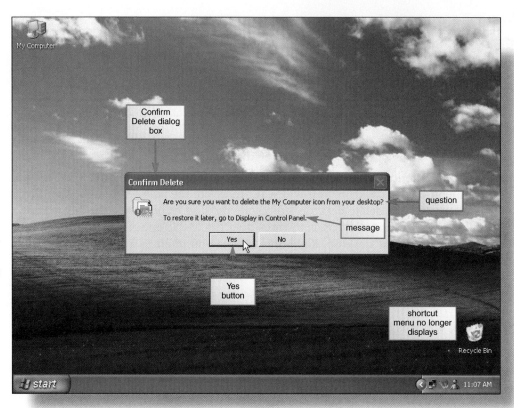

FIGURE 1-44

3 **Click the Yes button.**

The Confirm Delete dialog box closes and the My Computer icon no longer displays on the desktop (Figure 1-45). The My Computer icon now is contained in the Recycle Bin.

1. Drag icon to Recycle Bin, click Yes button
2. Right-click icon, click Delete, click Yes button

FIGURE 1-45

In Figure 1-43 on page WIN 1.37, the My Computer icon remains in its original location on the desktop and the shortcut menu contains two commands, Move Here and Cancel. The **Move Here command** in bold (dark) font identifies what would happen if you were to drag the My Computer icon with the left mouse button. If you click Move Here on the shortcut menu shown, Windows XP will move the icon from its current location to the new location. If you click Cancel, the operation will be terminated and the **Cancel command** will reset anything you have done during the operation.

In Figure 1-44, the Confirm Delete dialog box contains the Yes button and the No button. Clicking the Yes button completes the operation and clicking the No button terminates the operation.

Although you can move icons by dragging with the primary (left) mouse button and by right-dragging with the secondary (right) mouse button, it is strongly suggested you right-drag because a menu displays and, in most cases, you can specify the exact operation you want to occur. When you drag using the left mouse button, a default operation takes place and that operation may not be the operation you intended to perform.

Summary of Mouse and Windows Operations

You have seen how to use the mouse to point, click, right-click, double-click, drag, and right-drag in order to accomplish certain tasks on the desktop. The use of a mouse is an important skill when using Windows XP. In addition, you have learned how to move around and use windows on the Windows XP desktop.

The Keyboard and Keyboard Shortcuts

The **keyboard** is an input device on which you manually key in, or type, data. Figure 1-46 shows the Microsoft Office keyboard designed specifically for use with Microsoft Office and the Internet. The Single Touch pad along the left side of the keyboard contains keys to browse the Internet, copy and paste text, and switch between applications. A scroll wheel allows you to quickly move within a document window. The Hot Keys along the top of the keyboard allow you to launch a Web browser or e-mail program, play multi-media, and adjust the system volume.

More **About**

The Microsoft Office Keyboard

When using the Single Touch pad, Microsoft Office users place their left hand on the pad and their right hand on the mouse. These hand positions allow them to get more work done in less time. They also report that when using Hot Keys they can increase productivity because they do not have to take their hand off the keyboard as frequently to use a mouse.

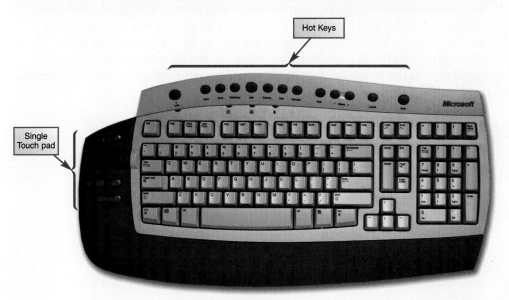

Hot Keys

Single Touch pad

FIGURE 1-46

Many tasks you accomplish with a mouse also can be accomplished using a keyboard. To perform tasks using the keyboard, you must understand the notation used to identify which keys to press. This notation is used throughout Windows XP to identify a **keyboard shortcut**.

Keyboard shortcuts consist of (1) pressing a single key (such as press the ENTER key); or (2) pressing and holding down one key and pressing a second key, as shown by two key names separated by a plus sign (such as press CTRL+ESC). For example, to obtain Help about Windows XP, you can press the F1 key and to display the Start menu, hold down the CTRL key and then press the ESC key (press CTRL+ESC).

Often, computer users will use keyboard shortcuts for operations they perform frequently. For example, many users find pressing the F1 key to launch Windows XP Help and Support easier than using the Start menu as shown later in this project. As a user, you probably will find the combination of keyboard and mouse operations that particularly suit you, but it is strongly recommended that generally you use the mouse.

Launching an Application Program

One of the basic tasks you can perform using Windows XP is to launch an application program. A **program** is a set of computer instructions that carries out a task on the computer. An **application program** is a program that allows you to accomplish a specific task for which that program is designed. For example, a **word processing program** is an application program that allows you to create written documents; a **presentation graphics program** is an application program that allows you to create graphic presentations for display on a computer; and a **Web browser program** is an application program that allows you to search for and display Web pages.

The **default Web browser program** (Internet Explorer) displays in the pinned items list on the Start menu shown in Figure 1-10 on page WIN 1.15. Because the default **Web browser** is selected during the installation of the Windows XP operating system, the default Web browser on your computer may be different. In addition, you can easily select another Web browser as the default Web browser. Another frequently used Web browser program is **MSN Explorer**.

Launching an Application Using the Start Menu

The most common activity performed on a computer is running an application program to accomplish tasks using the computer. You can launch an application program by using the Start menu. To illustrate the use of the Start menu to launch an application program, the default Web browser program (Internet Explorer) will be launched. Perform the following steps to launch Internet Explorer using the Internet command on the Start menu.

Steps To Launch a Program Using the Start Menu

1 **Click the Start button on the taskbar and then point to Internet on the pinned items list on the Start menu.**

The Start menu displays (Figure 1-47). The pinned items list on the Start menu contains the **Internet command** to launch the default Web browser program and the name of the default Web browser program (Internet Explorer). The default Web browser program on your computer may be different.

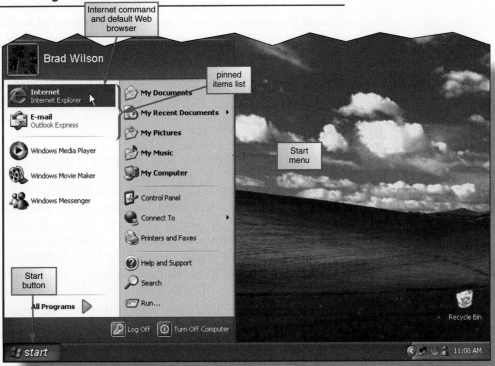

FIGURE 1-47

2 **Click Internet.**

Windows XP launches the Internet Explorer program by displaying the Welcome to MSN.com – Microsoft Internet Explorer window, displaying the MSN home page in the window, and adding a recessed button on the taskbar (Figure 1-48). The URL for the Web page displays in the Address bar. Because you can select the default Web browser and the Web page to display when you launch the Web browser, the Web page that displays on your desktop may be different.

3 **Click the Close button in the Microsoft Internet Explorer window.**

The Microsoft Internet Explorer window closes.

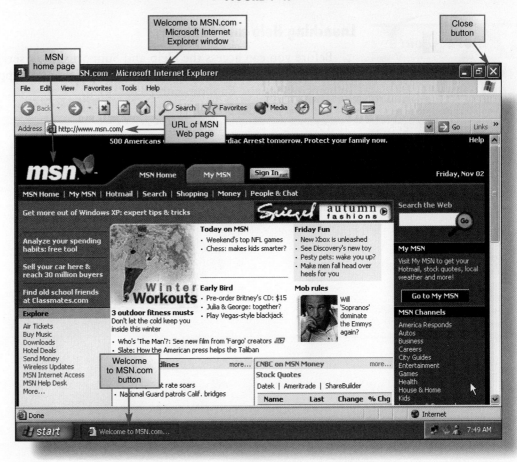

FIGURE 1-48

Any computer connected to the Internet that contains Web pages you can reference is called a **Web site**. The **MSN.com Web site**, one of millions of Web sites around the world, is stored on a computer operated by Microsoft Corporation and can be accessed using a Web browser. The Welcome to MSN.com **Web page** shown in Figure 1-48 on the previous page is the first Web page you see when you access the MSN.com Web site and is, therefore, referred to as a **home page**, or **start page**.

After you have launched a Web browser, you can use the program to search for and display additional Web pages located on different Web sites around the world.

Using Windows Help and Support

One of the more powerful Windows XP features is Help and Support. Help and Support is available when using Windows XP or when using any application program running under Windows XP. This feature is designed to assist you in using Windows XP or the various application programs.

Help and Support brings together the Help features that were available in previous versions of Windows (Search, Index, and Favorites) with the online Help features found on the Microsoft Web site. Help and Support includes access to articles in the Microsoft Knowledge Base, communication with Windows XP newsgroups, and troubleshooting solutions.

Help and Support also includes tools that allow you to view general information about the computer, update changes to the operating system, restore the computer to a previous state without losing data files, and permit an individual at another computer to connect to your computer and walk you through the solution to a problem.

Launching Help and Support

Before you can access the Help and Support Center services, you must launch Help and Support. One method of launching Help and Support uses the Start menu. To launch Help and Support, complete the following steps.

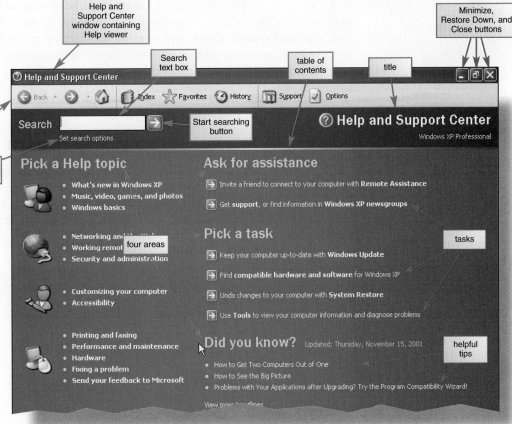

Steps To Launch Help and Support

1 **Click the Start button on the taskbar and then point to Help and Support on the Start menu.**

Windows XP displays the Start menu and highlights the Help and Support command (Figure 1-49).

FIGURE 1-49

2 **Click Help and Support and then click the Maximize button on the Help and Support Center title bar.**

*The Help and Support Center window opens and maximizes (Figure 1-50). The window contains the Help viewer. The **Help viewer** includes the navigation toolbar, Search text box and Set search options link, and table of contents. The **table of contents** contains four areas (Pick a Help topic, Ask for assistance, Pick a task, and Did you know?).*

Other Ways

1. Press F1
2. Press CTRL+ESC, press H
3. Press WINDOWS+F1 (WINDOWS key on Microsoft Natural keyboard)

FIGURE 1-50

The Help and Support Center title bar shown in Figure 1-50 on the previous page contains a Minimize button, Restore Down button, and Close button. You can minimize or restore the Help and Support Center window as needed and also close the Help and Support Center window.

The navigation toolbar displays below the title bar. The **navigation toolbar** allows you to navigate through Help topics and pages, browse and save Help topics and pages, view previously saved Help topics and pages, get online support for questions and problems, and customize the Help viewer. An icon identifies each button on the **navigation toolbar**. Six buttons contain a text label (Back, Index, Favorites, History, Support, and Options). The buttons on the navigation toolbar on your computer may be different.

The area below the navigation toolbar contains the Search text box and Start searching button used to search for Help, the Set search options link to set the criteria for searching the Help and Support Center, and the window's title (Help and Support Center).

The **table of contents** contains four areas. The **Pick a Help topic area** contains four category groups. A unique icon identifies each group. Clicking a category in a group displays a list of subcategories and Help topics related to the category.

The **Ask for assistance area** contains two tasks. The first task (**Remote Assistance**) allows another individual at another computer to connect and control your computer while helping to solve a problem. The second task (**Windows XP newsgroups**) allows you to obtain Help from product support experts or discuss your questions with other Windows XP users in newsgroups.

The **Pick a task area** contains four tasks. The first task (**Windows Update**) allows you to access a catalog of items such as device drivers, security fixes, critical updates, the latest Help files, and Internet products that you can download to keep your computer up-to-date. The second task (**compatible hardware and software**) allows you to search for hardware and software that is compatible with Windows XP. The third task (**System Restore**) allows you to store the current state of your computer and restore your computer to that state without losing important information. The fourth task (**Tools**) contains a collection of 15 helpful tools to keep your computer running smoothly. The **Did you know? area** is updated daily with helpful tips for using Windows XP.

Browsing for Help Topics in the Table of Contents

After launching Help and Support, the next step is to find the Help topic in which you are interested. Assume you want to know more about finding information using the Help and Support Center. Perform the following steps to use the table of contents to find a Help topic that describes how to find what you need in the Help and Support Center.

More About

The Table of Contents

The table of contents in Windows XP resembles the Contents sheet in previous versions of Windows. To display the Contents sheet you had to click the Contents tab in the Help window. Now, the table of contents displays in a prominent position and contains links to online Help and Support topics.

Steps To Browse for Help Topics in the Table of Contents

1 **Point to Windows basics in the Pick a Help topic area.**

The mouse pointer changes to a hand icon when positioned on the Windows basics category and the category is underlined (Figure 1-51).

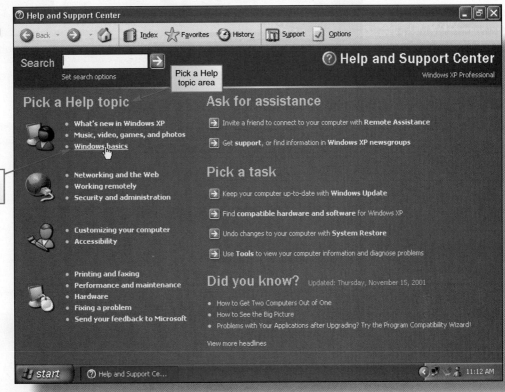

FIGURE 1-51

2 **Click Windows basics and then point to Tips for using Help.**

The navigation pane and topic pane display in the Help and Support Center window (Figure 1-52). The Windows basics area in the navigation pane contains five categories and the underlined Tips for using Help category. The See Also area contains four Help topics. The topic pane contains the Help and Support toolbar and the Windows basics page.

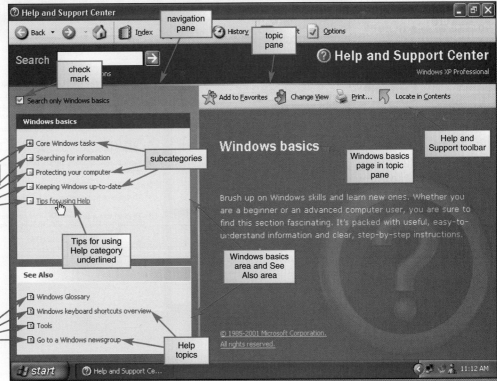

FIGURE 1-52

3 **Click Tips for using Help and then point to Find what you need in Help and Support Center in the topic pane.**

Windows XP highlights the Tips for using Help category in the Windows basics area, displays the Tips for using Help page in the topic pane, and underlines the Find what you need in Help and Support Center task (Figure 1-53). The Add to Favorites button and Print button on the Help and Support Center toolbar are dimmed to indicate the page cannot be added to the favorites list or printed.

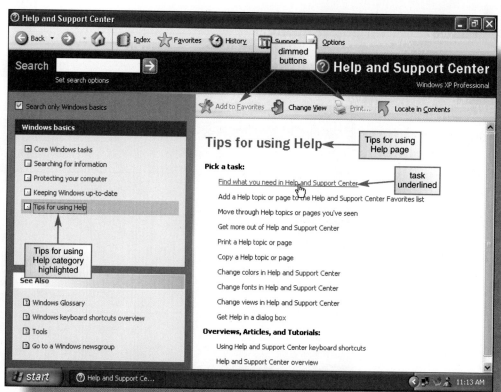

FIGURE 1-53

4 **Click Find what you need in Help and Support Center and then read the information in the To find what you need in Help and Support Center topic in the topic pane.**

Windows XP removes the dotted rectangle surrounding the Tips for using Help category in the Windows basics area and displays the To find what you need in Help and Support Center topic in the topic pane (Figure 1-54). Clicking the Related Topics link displays a list of related Help topics.

1. Press TAB until category or topic is highlighted, press ENTER, repeat for each category or topic

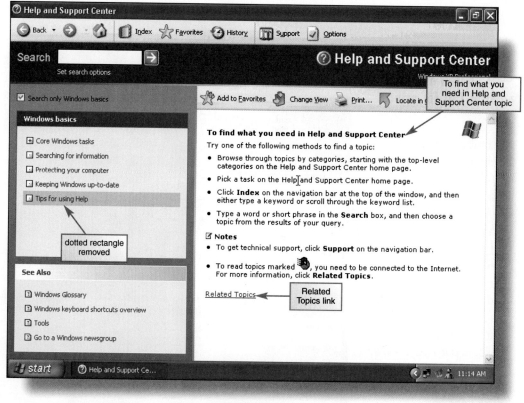

FIGURE 1-54

Using Windows Help and Support • WIN 1.47

PROJECT 1

The check mark in the **Search only Windows basics check box** shown in Figure 1-52 on page WIN 1.45 indicates that when searching for a Help topic using the Search text box, only the topics in the Windows basics category will be searched.

In the Windows basics area, the **plus sign** in the small box to the left of the Core Windows tasks category indicates the category contains subcategories but the subcategories do not display in the area. Clicking the box with the plus sign displays a list of subcategories below the Core Windows category. A **bullet** in a small box indicates a category. Clicking the bullet within a small box displays a list of tasks in the topic pane.

Each of the four Help topics in the See Also area is identified by a question mark in a document icon. The **question mark** indicates a Help topic without further subdivision.

The Help and Support Center toolbar in the topic pane shown in Figure 1-52 contains four buttons. An icon and text label identify each button on the toolbar. The buttons allow you to add a Help topic to the favorites list, display only the Help and Support Center toolbar and topic pane in the Help and Support Center window, print a Help topic in the topic pane, and locate a Help topic in the topic pane in the table of contents.

In the future, if you want to return to a favorite Help topic, click the Favorites button on the **navigation toolbar,** click the topic name in the Favorites area, and then click the Display button. The topic will display in the topic pane of the Help and Support Center window. The steps to display a topic are illustrated later in this project.

Using the Help and Support Center Index

A second method of finding answers to your questions about Windows XP is to use the Help and Support Center Index. The **Help and Support Center Index** contains a list of index entries, each of which references one or more Help topics. Assume you want more information about home networking. Perform the steps on the next page to learn more about home networking.

Bookmarks

After browsing for a Help topic, you may want to bookmark the topic for easy retrieval in the future. To bookmark a topic, click the Add to Favorites button on Help and Support and then click the OK button in the Help and Support Center dialog box. If you want to return to the topic, click the Favorites button on the navigation toolbar, click the topic name in the Favorites area, and then click the Display button.

Steps | **To Search for Help Topics Using the Index**

1 **Click the Index button on the navigation toolbar, type** home networking **in the Type in the keyword to find text box, and then point to components in the home network in the list box.**

The Index area, containing the Type in the keyword to find text box, list box, and Display button, displays in the navigation pane and the Index page displays in the topic pane (Figure 1-55). When you type an entry in the text box, the list of index entries in the list box automatically scrolls and the entry you type (home networking) is highlighted in the list. Several entries display indented below the home networking entry.

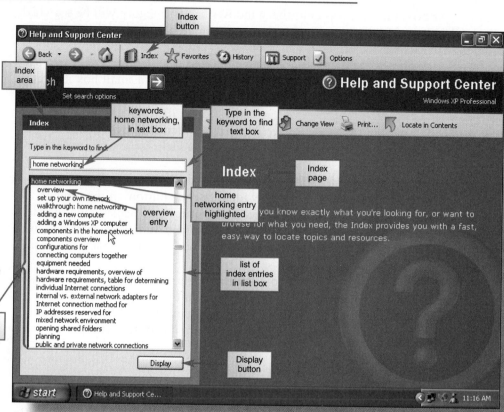

FIGURE 1-55

2 **Click components in the home network in the list box and then point to the Display button.**

Windows XP displays the components in the home network entry in the text box and highlights the components in the home network entry in the list box (Figure 1-56). The yellow outline surrounding the Display button indicates the button is recessed.

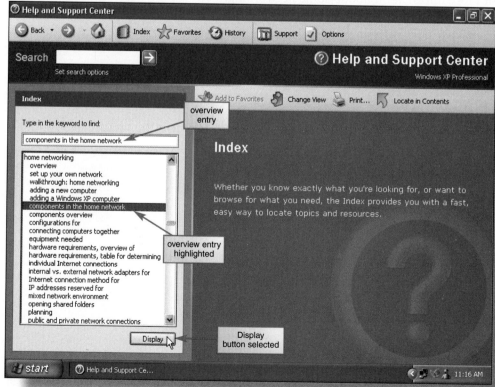

FIGURE 1-56

3 Click the Display button.

The Home and small office networking components overview topic displays in the topic pane (Figure 1-57). The topic contains an overview of home and small office networking components. Additional information is available by using the vertical scroll bar in the topic pane.

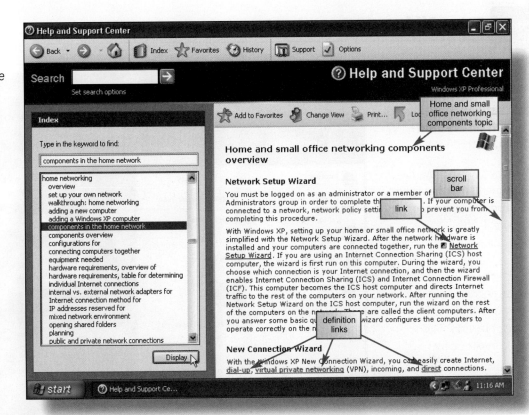

FIGURE 1-57

In Figure 1-57, the dial-up, virtual private networking, and direct links are underlined and display in green font to indicate that clicking the link will display its definition. To remove the definition, click anywhere off the definition. Although not visible in Figure 1-57, other links, such as the Related Topics link, display at the bottom of the page, underlined, and in blue font. Clicking the Related Topics link displays a pop-up window that contains topics related to the home or small office network overview.

After using the Help and Support Center, normally you will close the Help and Support Center. To close the Help and Support Center, complete the following step.

TO CLOSE THE HELP AND SUPPORT CENTER

1 Click the Close button on the title bar of the Help and Support Center window.

Windows XP closes the Help and Support Center window.

Logging Off and Turning Off the Computer

After completing your work with Windows XP, you should close your user account by logging off from the computer. Logging off from the computer closes any open applications, allows you to save any unsaved documents, ends the Windows XP session, and makes the computer available for other users. Perform the steps on the next page to log off from the computer.

Other Ways

1. Press ALT+N, type keyword, press DOWN ARROW until topic is highlighted, press ALT+D (or ENTER)

More *About*

Logging Off the Computer

Some users of Windows XP have turned off their computers without following the log off procedure only to find data they thought they had stored on disk was lost. Because of the way Windows XP writes data on the disk, it is important you log off the computer so you do not lose your work.

Steps To Log Off from the Computer

1 **Click the Start button on the taskbar and then point to Log Off on the Start menu.**

Windows XP displays the Start menu and highlights the Log Off command (Figure 1-58).

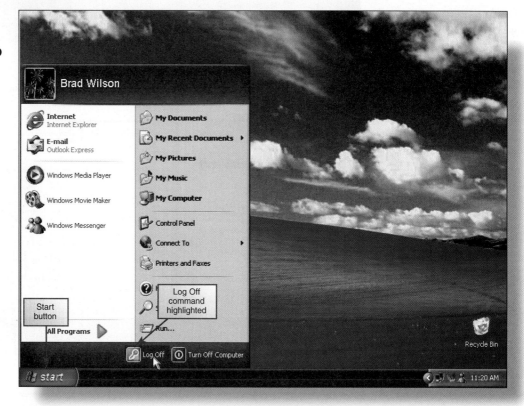

FIGURE 1-58

2 **Click Log Off. Point to the Log Off button in the Log Off Windows dialog box.**

The Log Off Windows dialog box displays (Figure 1-59). The dialog box contains three buttons (Switch User, Log Off, and Cancel). Pointing to the Log Off button changes the color of the button to light orange and displays the Log Off balloon. The balloon contains the balloon name, Log Off, and the text, Closes your programs and ends your Windows session. The Cancel button is hidden behind the balloon.

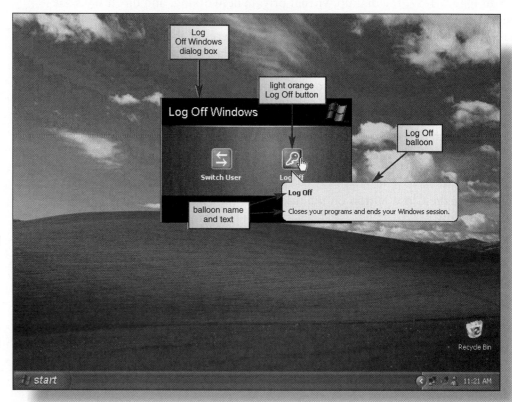

FIGURE 1-59

3 **Click the Log Off button.**

Windows XP logs off from the computer and displays the Welcome screen (Figure 1-60). A message displays below the Brad Wilson name on the Welcome screen to indicate the user has unread e-mail messages.

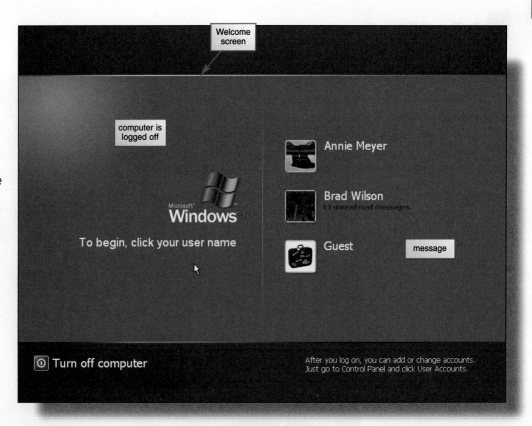

FIGURE 1-60

While Windows XP is logging off, a blue screen containing the word, Welcome, displays on the desktop and the messages, Logging off..., and Saving your settings..., display on the screen momentarily. The blue screen closes and the Welcome screen (Figure 1-60) displays on the desktop. At this point, another user can log on.

If you accidentally click Log Off on the Start menu as shown in Figure 1-58 and you do not want to log off, click the Cancel button in the Log Off Windows dialog box to return to normal Windows XP operation.

After logging off, you also may want to turn off the computer using the **Turn Off Computer link** on the Welcome screen. Turning off the computer shuts down Windows XP so you can turn off the power to the computer. Many computers turn the power off automatically. If you are sure you want to turn off the computer, perform the steps on the next page. If you are not sure about turning off the computer, read the steps on the next page without actually performing them.

Steps **To Turn Off the Computer**

1 **Point to the Turn off computer link on the Welcome screen.**

Pointing to the Turn off computer link underlines the Turn off computer link (Figure 1-61).

FIGURE 1-61

2 **Click Turn off computer.**

The Welcome screen darkens and the Turn off computer dialog box displays (Figure 1-62). The dialog box contains four buttons (Stand By, Turn Off, Restart, and Cancel). The buttons allow you to perform different operations, such as placing the computer in stand by mode (Stand By), shutting down Windows XP (Turn Off), restarting the computer (Restart), and canceling the process of shutting down Windows XP (Cancel).

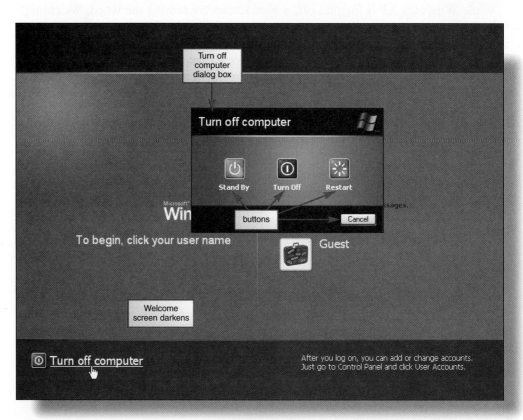

FIGURE 1-62

3 Point to the Turn Off button in the Turn off computer dialog box.

The color of the Turn Off button changes to light red and the Turn Off balloon displays (Figure 1-63). The balloon contains the balloon name, Turn Off, and the text, Shuts down Windows so that you can safely turn off the computer.

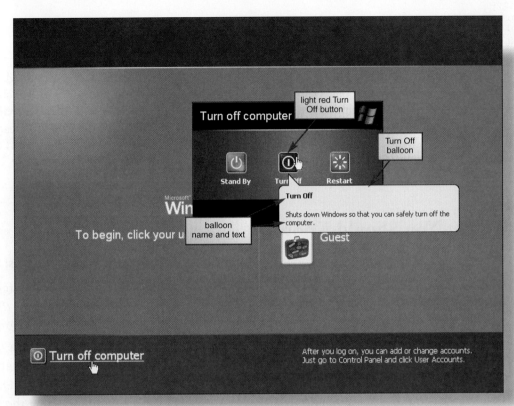

4 Click the Turn Off button.

Windows XP is shut down.

FIGURE 1-63

Other Ways

1. Press CTRL+ESC, press U, use ARROW KEYS to select Turn Off, press ENTER

2. Press ALT+F4, use ARROW KEYS to select Turn Off, press ENTER

While Windows XP is shutting down, a blue screen containing the word, Welcome, displays on the desktop and the message, Windows is shutting down..., displays momentarily. At this point, you can turn off the computer. When shutting down Windows XP, you should never turn off the computer before these messages display.

If you accidentally click Turn off computer on the Welcome screen as shown in Figure 1-61 and you do not want to shut down Windows XP, click the Cancel button in the Turn off computer dialog box in Figure 1-62 to return to normal Windows XP operation.

CASE PERSPECTIVE SUMMARY

While continuing to answer questions about Windows XP in the workplace, you spent nearly every free moment in the two weeks prior to the seminar learning about the newly installed operating system. Then, the daily training sessions kept you busy for the following three months. You taught 35 workshops and trained all of the 324 employees in the company. Your supervisor, who attended the Windows XP seminar, complimented your success by giving you a sizable pay raise and time off to attend the annual Comdex computer convention in Las Vegas, Nevada.

Project Summary

Project 1 illustrated the Microsoft Windows XP graphical user interface. You launched Windows XP, logged on to the computer, learned the parts of the desktop, and learned to point, click, right-click, double-click, drag, and right-drag. You opened, minimized, maximized, restored, and closed a Windows XP window, as well as learned how to launch an application. Using the table of contents, Index, Search, and Favorites, you obtained Help about Microsoft Windows XP and bookmarked important Help topics. You logged off from the computer using the Log Off Command on the Start menu and then shut down Windows XP using the Turn off computer link on the Welcome screen.

What You Should Know

Having completed this project, you now should be able to perform the following tasks:

▶ Add an Icon to the Desktop *(WIN 1.18)*
▶ Browse for Help Topics in the Table of Contents *(WIN 1.45)*
▶ Close a Window *(WIN 1.27, WIN 1.37)*
▶ Close the Help and Support Center *(WIN 1.49)*
▶ Collapse an Area *(WIN 1.35)*
▶ Delete a Desktop Icon by Right-Dragging *(WIN 1.37)*
▶ Display the Start Menu *(WIN 1.14)*
▶ Expand an Area *(WIN 1.31)*
▶ Launch a Program Using the Start Menu *(WIN 1.41)*
▶ Launch Help and Support *(WIN 1.43)*

▶ Log Off from the Computer *(WIN 1.50)*
▶ Log On to the Computer *(WIN 1.12)*
▶ Maximize and Restore a Window *(WIN 1.25)*
▶ Minimize and Redisplay a Window *(WIN 1.23)*
▶ Move a Window by Dragging *(WIN 1.30)*
▶ Open a Window Using a Desktop Icon *(WIN 1.21)*
▶ Open a Window Using the Start Menu *(WIN 1.28)*
▶ Resize a Window *(WIN 1.36)*
▶ Scroll Using Scroll Arrows *(WIN 1.32)*
▶ Search for Help Topics Using the Index *(WIN 1.48)*
▶ Size a Window by Dragging *(WIN 1.34)*
▶ Turn Off the Computer *(WIN 1.52)*

Learn It Online

Instructions: To complete the Learn It Online exercises, launch your Web browser using the steps on pages WIN 1.46 and WIN 1.47, click the Address box, enter scsite.com/winxp/exs.htm, and then press the ENTER key. When the Windows XP Learn It Online page displays, follow the instructions in the exercises below.

1 Project Reinforcement TF, MC, and SA

Below Windows XP Project 1, click the Project Reinforcement link. Print the quiz by clicking Print on the File menu. Answer each question. Write your first and last name at the top of each page, and then hand in the printout to your instructor.

2 Flash Cards

Below Windows XP Project 1, click the Flash Cards link. When Flash Cards displays, read the instructions. Type 20 (or a number specified by your instructor) in the Number of Playing Cards text box, type your name in the Name text box, and then click the Flip Card button. When the flash card displays, read the question and then click the Answer box arrow to select an answer. Flip through Flash Cards. Click Print on the File menu to print the last flash card if your score is 15 (75%) correct or greater and then hand it in to your instructor. If your score is less than 15 (75%) correct, then redo this exercise by clicking the Replay button.

3 Practice Test

Below Windows XP Project 1, click the Practice Test link. Answer each question, enter your first and last name at the bottom of the page, and then click the Grade Test button. When the graded practice test displays on your screen, click Print on the File menu to print a hard copy. Continue to take practice tests until you score 80% or better. Hand in a printout of the final practice test to your instructor.

4 Who Wants to Be a Computer Genius?

Below Windows XP Project 1, click the Computer Genius link. Read the instructions, enter your first and last name at the bottom of the page, and then click the Play button. Hand in a printout of your score to your instructor.

5 Wheel of Terms

Below Windows XP Project 1, click the Wheel of Terms link. Read the instructions, and then enter your first and last name and your school name. Click the Play button. Hand in a printout of your score to your instructor.

6 Crossword Puzzle Challenge

Below Windows XP Project 1, click the Crossword Puzzle Challenge link. Read the instructions, and then enter your first and last name. Click the Play button. Work the crossword puzzle. When you are finished, click the Submit button. When the crossword puzzle redisplays, click the Print button. Hand in the printout.

7 Tips and Tricks

Below Windows XP Project 1, click the Tips and Tricks link. Click a topic that pertains to Project 1. Right-click the information and then click Print on the shortcut menu. Construct a brief example of what the information relates to in Windows XP to confirm that you understand how to use the tip or trick. Hand in the example and printed information.

online

8 Newsgroups

Below Windows XP Project 1, click the Newsgroups link. Click a topic that pertains to Project 1. Print three comments. Hand in the comments to your instructor.

9 Expanding Your Horizons

Below Windows XP Project 1, click the Expanding Your Horizons link. Click a topic that pertains to Project 1. Print the information. Construct a brief example of what the information relates to in Windows XP to confirm that you understand the contents of the article. Hand in the example and printed information to your instructor.

10 Search Sleuth

Below Windows XP Project 1, click the Search Sleuth link. To search for a term that pertains to this project, select a term below the Project 1 title and then use the Google search engine at google.com (or any major search engine) to display and print two Web pages that present information on the term. Hand in the printouts to your instructor.

Use Help

1 Using the Help and Support Center

Instructions: Use Help and Support Center and a computer to perform the following tasks.

Part 1: *Using the Question Mark Button*

1. If necessary, launch Microsoft Windows XP and log on to the computer.
2. Right-click an open area of the desktop to display a shortcut menu.
3. Click Properties on the shortcut menu to display the Display Properties dialog box.
4. Click the Desktop tab in the Display Properties dialog box.
5. Click the Help button on the title bar. The mouse pointer changes to a block arrow with a question mark.
6. Click the list box in the Desktop sheet. A pop-up window displays explaining the list box. Read the information in the pop-up window and summarize the function of the list box.

   _____

7. Click an open area of the Desktop sheet to remove the pop-up window.
8. Click the Help button on the title bar and then click the Customize Desktop button. A pop-up window displays explaining what happens when you click this button. Read the information in the pop-up window and summarize the function of the button.

   _____

9. Click an open area in the Desktop sheet to remove the pop-up window.
10. Click the Help button on the title bar and then click the monitor icon in the Desktop sheet. A pop-up window displays explaining the function of the monitor. Read the information in the pop-up window and summarize the function of the monitor.

    _____

11. Click an open area in the Desktop sheet to remove the pop-up window.
12. Click the Help button on the title bar and then click the Cancel button. A pop-up window displays explaining what happens when you click the button. Read the information in the pop-up window and summarize the function of the Cancel button.

    _____

13. Click an open area in the Desktop sheet to remove the pop-up window.
14. Click the Cancel button in the Display Properties dialog box.

Part 2: *Finding What's New in Windows XP*

1. Click the Start button and then click Help and Support on the Start menu.
2. Click the Maximize button on the Help and Support Center title bar.
3. Click What's new in Windows XP in the navigation pane.
4. Click What's new topics in the navigation pane. Ten topics display in the topic pane.
5. Click What's new on your desktop in the topic pane.
6. Click Start menu (or the plus sign in the small box preceding Start menu) to expand the entry. Read the information about the Start menu.

Use Help

7. Click the Using the Start menu link.
8. Click the Print button on the Help and Support toolbar to print the topic. Click the Print button in the Print dialog box.
9. Scroll the topic pane to display the Related Topics link. Click the Related Topics link to display a pop-up window containing three related topics. List the three topics.

_____

_____

_____

10. Click Display a program at the top of the Start menu in the pop-up window.
11. Click the Print button on the Help and Support toolbar to print the topic. Click the Print button in the Print dialog box.

Part 3: *Viewing Windows XP Articles*

1. Click Windows XP articles: Walk through ways to use your PC in the What's new in Windows XP area in the navigation pane. A list of overviews, articles, and tutorials displays in the topic pane.
2. Click Walkthrough: Making music in the topic pane. Read the Making music article in the topic pane. List four ways in which you can use Windows XP musically.

_____

_____

_____

_____

3. Click Play music in the Making Music area. Scroll to display the Display details about a CD area. List the three steps to display details about a CD.

_____

_____

_____

4. Scroll to the top of the window to display the Making Music area.
5. Click Create CDs in the Making Music area. Scroll to display the steps to burn your own CD. List the six steps to burn a CD.

_____

_____

_____

_____

_____

_____

6. Read other articles of interest to you in the Making music area.
7. Click the Close button in the Help and Support Center window.

Use Help

2 Using Windows Help and Support to Obtain Help

Instructions: Use Help and Support Center and a computer to perform the following tasks.

1. Find Help about Help and Support Center keyboard shortcuts by exploring the Windows keyboard shortcuts overview in the Accessibility category in the table of contents.
   a. What general keyboard shortcut is used to display the Start menu?

   _____

   b. What general keyboard shortcut is used to display the shortcut menu for an active window?

   _____

   c. What general keyboard shortcut is used to view the properties for a selected item?

   _____

   d. What dialog box keyboard shortcut is used to move backward through options?

   _____

   e. What dialog box keyboard shortcut is used to display Help?

   _____

   f. What natural keyboard shortcut is used to display or hide the Start menu?

   _____

   g. What natural keyboard shortcut is used to open the My Computer window?

   _____

2. Use the Help Index feature to answer the following questions in the spaces provided.
   a. How do you reduce computer screen flicker?

   _____

   b. What dialog box do you use to change the appearance of the mouse pointer?

   _____

   c. How do you minimize all windows?

   _____

   d. What is a server?

   _____

3. Use the Search text box in the Help and Support Center window to answer the following questions in the spaces provided.
   a. How can you reduce all open windows on the desktop to taskbar buttons?

   _____

   b. How do you launch a program using the Run command?

   _____

   c. What are the steps to add a toolbar to the taskbar?

   _____

   d. What wizard do you use to remove unwanted desktop icons?

   _____

   e. Close the Help and Support Center window.

In the Lab

d. What is contained in the notification area? _____

e. How does Windows keep the taskbar tidy? _____

f. What does a right-facing arrow on a Start menu command signify? _____
   _____

g. In which folders are text, image, and music files placed? _____
   _____

h. What does the Restore Down button do? _____

i. What appears when a program needs some information from you before it can complete a command?
   _____

j. What do you use to set up user accounts? _____

k. Where do you go when you want to interrupt your Windows session and let someone else use the computer? _____

4. Click the Skip Intro button in the lower corner of the desktop to skip the introduction to the Windows XP tour.

5. If available, click the Best for Business button and listen to the narration.

6. Click the red Safe and Easy Personal Computing button and listen to the narration.

7. Click the green Unlock the World of Digital Media button and listen to the narration.

8. Click the blue The Connected Home and Office button and listen to the narration.

9. Click the red Exit Tour button on the desktop to exit the Windows XP tour.

10. Click the Close button in the Help and Support center window.

11. You have completed this lab assignment.

Part 3: *Taking the Windows XP Tour without Sound or Animation*

1. Click the Play the non-animated tour that features text and images only button in the Windows XP Tour dialog box and then click the Next button.

2. Click the Start Here button to read about the basics of the Windows XP operating system.

3. Scroll the Windows XP Basics window and read the paragraph below the Windows Desktop heading. Click the Next button to display the next topic.

4. Scroll the Windows XP Basics window and read the paragraphs below the Icons heading. Answer the following questions.
   a. What icon displays on the desktop the first time you launch Windows? _____
   b. Does deleting a shortcut icon affect the actual program or file? _____

5. Click the Next button to display the next topic. Scroll the Windows XP Basics window and read the paragraphs below the Taskbar heading. Answer the following question.
   a. Where is the notification area located? _____

6. Click the Next button to display the next topic. Scroll the Windows XP Basics window and read the paragraphs below the Start Menu heading. Answer the following question.
   a. What does a right-facing arrow mean? _____

7. Click the Next button to display the next topic. Scroll the Windows XP Basics window and read the paragraph, below the Files and Folder heading. Answer the following question.
   a. In which folders are text, image, and music files placed?
   _____

(continued)

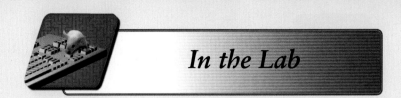

In the Lab

Taking the Windows XP Tour *(continued)*

8. Click the Next button to display the next topic. Scroll the Windows XP Basics window and read the paragraphs below the Windows heading. Answer the following question.
   a. What displays if a program needs some information from you before it can complete a command?

   _____

9. Click the Next button to display the next topic. Scroll the Windows XP Basics window and read the paragraphs below the Control Panel heading. Answer the following questions.
   a. What Windows feature do you use to customize computer settings? _____
   b. Where is this feature located? _____

10. Click the Next button to display the next topic. Scroll the Windows XP Basics window and read the paragraphs below the Ending Your Session heading. Answer the following question.
    a. What do you do when you want to interrupt your Windows session and let someone else use the computer? _____

11. Click the Next button repeatedly to display the topics in the remaining sections of the Windows XP tour.
12. Click the Close button in the window to end the tour.
13. Click the Close button in the Help and Support Center window.
14. You have completed this lab assignment.

3 Launching and Using the Internet Explorer Application

Instructions: Perform the following steps to launch the Internet Explorer application.

Part 1: *Launching the Internet Explorer Application*

1. If necessary, launch Microsoft Windows XP and log on to the computer.
2. If necessary, connect to the Internet.
3. Click the Start button and then click Internet in the pinned items list on the Start menu. Maximize the Microsoft Internet Explorer window.
4. If the Address bar does not display below the Standard Buttons toolbar in the Microsoft Internet Explorer window, click View on the menu bar, point to Toolbars, and then click Address bar on the Toolbars submenu.

Part 2: *Entering a URL in the Address Bar*

1. Click the URL in the Address bar to highlight the URL.
2. Type www.microsoft.com in the Address bar and then press the ENTER key.
3. Answer the following questions.
   a. What URL displays in the Address bar? _____
   b. What window title displays on the title bar? _____

   _____

In the Lab

4. If necessary, scroll the Web page to view the contents of the Web page. List five links (underlined text) that are shown on this Web page.

   _____

   _____

5. Click any link on the Web page. What link did you click? _____

6. Describe the Web page that displayed when you clicked the link? _____

   _____

7. Click the Print button on the Standard Buttons toolbar to print the Web page.

Part 3: *Entering a URL in the Address Bar*

1. Click the URL in the Address bar to highlight the URL.
2. Type `www.disney.com` in the Address bar and then press the ENTER key.
3. What window title displays on the title bar? _____
4. Scroll the Web page to view the contents of the Web page. Do any graphic images display on the Web page?

   _____

5. Pointing to an image on a Web page and having the mouse pointer change to a hand indicates the image is a link. Does the Web page include an image that is a link? _____
   If so, describe the image. _____

6. Click the image to display another Web page. What window title displays on the title bar?

   _____

7. Click the Print button on the Standard Buttons toolbar to print the Web page.

Part 4: *Displaying Previously Displayed Web Pages*

1. Click the Back button on the Standard Buttons toolbar. What Web page displays?

   _____

2. Click the Back button on the Standard Buttons toolbar twice. What Web page displays?

   _____

3. Click the Forward button on the Standard Buttons toolbar. What Web page displays?

   _____

Part 5: *Entering a URL in the Address Bar*

1. Click the URL in the Address bar to highlight the URL.
2. Type `www.scsite.com` in the Address bar and then press the ENTER key.
3. Scroll the Web page to display the Operating Systems link.
4. Click the Operating Systems link.
5. Click the textbook title of your Windows XP textbook.
6. Click the Steve's Cool Sites link on the Web page.
7. Click any links that are of interest to you. Which link did you like the best? _____
8. Use the Back button or Forward button to display the Web site you like the best.
9. Click the Print button on the Standard Buttons toolbar to print the Web page.
10. Click the Close button on the Microsoft Internet Explorer title bar.

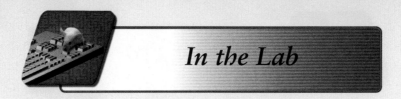

In the Lab

4 Launching an Application

Instructions: Perform the following steps to launch the Notepad application using the Start menu and create the homework list shown in Figure 1-64. **Notepad** is a popular application program available with Windows XP that allows you to create, save, and print simple text documents.

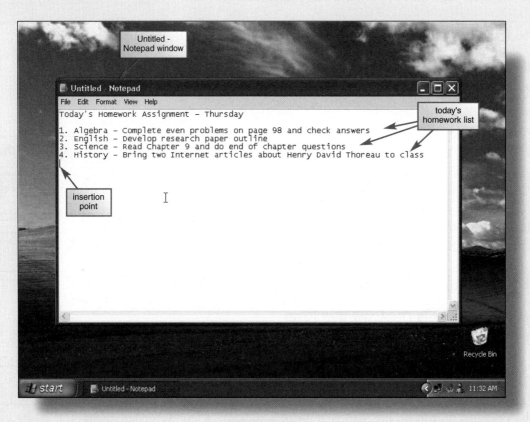

FIGURE 1-64

Part 1: *Launching the Notepad Application*

1. If necessary, launch Microsoft Windows XP and log on to the computer.
2. Click the Start button.
3. Point to All Programs on the Start menu, point to Accessories on the All Programs submenu, and click Notepad on the Accessories submenu. The Untitled - Notepad window displays and an insertion point (flashing vertical line) displays in the blank area below the menu bar.

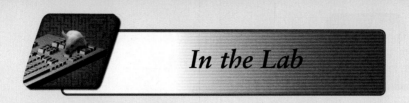

In the Lab

Part 2: *Creating a Document Using Notepad*

1. Type Today's Homework Assignments - Thursday and then press the ENTER key twice.
2. Type 1. Algebra - Complete even problems on page 98 and check answers and then press the ENTER key.
3. Type 2. English - Develop research paper outline and then press the ENTER key.
4. Type 3. Science - Read chapter 9 and do end of chapter questions and then press the ENTER key.
5. Type 4. History - Bring two Internet articles about Henry David Thoreau to class and then press the ENTER key.

Part 3: *Printing the Today's Homework Document*

1. Click File on the menu bar and then click Print. Click the Print button in the Print dialog box to print the document.
2. Retrieve the printed Today's Homework list from the printer.

Part 4: *Closing the Notepad Window*

1. Click the Close button on the Notepad title bar.
2. Click the No button in the Notepad dialog box to not save the Today's Homework document.

Cases and Places

The difficulty of these case studies varies:
▶ are the least difficult; ▶▶ are more difficult; and ▶▶▶ are the most difficult.

1 ▶ Technical support is an important consideration when installing and using an operating system or an application software program. The ability to obtain a valid answer to a question at the moment you have the question can be the difference between a frustrating incident and a positive experience. Using XP Help and Support, the Internet, or another research facility, write a brief report on the options that are available for obtaining Help and technical support while using Windows XP.

2 ▶ The Windows XP operating system can be installed only on computers found in the Windows XP hardware compatibility list. Locate three older personal computers. Look for them in your school's computer lab, at a local business, or in your house. Use Help and Support and the Internet to find the Microsoft Web page that contains the Windows XP hardware compatibility list. Check each computer against the list and write a brief report summarizing your results.

3 ▶▶ Early personal computer operating systems were adequate, but they were not user-friendly and had few advanced features. Over the past several years, however, personal computer operating systems have become increasingly easy to use, and some now offer features once available only on mainframe computers. Using the Internet, a library, or other research facility, write a brief report on three personal computer operating systems. Describe the systems, pointing out their similarities and differences. Discuss the advantages and disadvantages of each. Finally, tell which operating system you would purchase and explain why.

4 ▶▶▶ In addition to Windows XP, Microsoft also sells the Windows 98 operating system. Some say Windows XP will replace Windows 98 in the future. Using the Internet, computer magazines, or other resources, prepare a brief report comparing and contrasting the operating systems. How do their graphical user interfaces compare? What features and commands are shared by both operating systems? Does either operating system have features or commands that the other operating system does not have? Explain whether you think Windows XP will replace Windows 98.

5 ▶▶▶ Because of the many important tasks an operating system performs, most businesses put a great deal of thought into choosing an operating system. Interview a person at a local business about the operating system it uses with its computers. Based on the interview, write a brief report on why the business chose that operating system, how satisfied it is with it, and under what circumstances it might consider switching to a different operating system.

Microsoft Windows XP

Using Windows XP Explorer

You will have mastered the material in this project when you can:

- Launch Microsoft Windows XP
- Launch Windows XP Explorer
- Expand drives and folders in Explorer
- Display files and folders in Explorer
- Display the contents of drives and folders in Explorer
- Launch an application program from Explorer
- Close folder expansions
- Copy, rename, and delete files in Explorer
- Close Explorer

Sue's Timeline of Events

August 12, 1990 -- Susan Hendrickson, an amateur fossil hunter discovers three huge bones jutting out of a cliff in South Dakota. They belong to the largest, most complete, and best preserved *T. rex* ever discovered. It was nicknamed Sue in honor of its discoverer.
(© Photos above provided courtesy of Black Hills Institute of Geological Research, Inc., Hill City, South Dakota. Photographer Peter Larson)

☐ Continue
☐ Back to Timeline

Road Trip

Exploring the Desktop

Road trips can lead to some exciting explorations. Scientist Sue Hendrickson and her traveling companions were cruising through the Black Hills of South Dakota in August 1990 on a fossil-hunting expedition. When their truck got a flat tire, her friends decided to go into town to get the flat fixed and to escape the summer heat briefly. Hendrickson stayed with the truck.

She hiked a short distance, scanned the area, and spotted some bone fragments on the ground. Then, she gazed upward toward the cliffs and located large bones jutting from the cliff walls. She scaled the rocks and saw the bones from a Tyrannosaurus rex dinosaur. When her friends returned, they confirmed her discovery and named the dinosaur "Sue" in her honor.

Today the dinosaur, Sue, resides in Chicago's Field Museum. She is the largest and most complete preserved

T. rex ever found. The more than 200 fossilized bones in the skeleton stand 13 feet high and 42 feet long. Scientists estimate that Sue weighed seven tons when alive and that she could eat 500 pounds of meat and bones in one bite.

Hendrickson joins the ranks of great explorers throughout the world. After Christopher Columbus's return to Spain from the famous 1492 voyage across the Atlantic, other European explorers began navigating to North America. These great adventurers from Portugal, Spain, Italy, France, and England ventured farther with each voyage. In 1497, John Cabot explored the coasts of Labrador, Newfoundland, and New England. Juan Ponce de León discovered Florida and part of the Yucatán Peninsula in the early 1500s. Hernán Cortés invaded Mexico in 1519 and then conquered the Aztecs.

Every age has produced explorers with an insatiable thirst for knowing what lies over the next hill: Sir Edmund Hillary, Junípero Serra, Louis Joliet, Amelia Earhart, Vasco Nuñez de Balboa, Sir Walter Raleigh, and Leif Ericsson. In the latter half of the twentieth century, Neil Armstrong and Buzz Aldrin led the way to the moon, Jacques Cousteau explored the wonders beneath the sea, and Robert Ballard discovered the resting place of the Titanic.

The increasing power and versatility of modern personal computers have given people the means to embark on these and other grand individual adventures. In this project, you will examine files, documents, and folders on your computer in a variety of ways. The application program provided with the operating system, Windows XP Explorer, and the My Computer window allow you to view hardware components on the computer and computer resources on a network, as well as organize the files and folders on the computer.

As a desktop explorer of the twenty-first century, you have the tools to navigate computer and network resources at the click of a mouse button using the best of the Windows operating systems developed to date. Fasten your seat belt and get ready to embark on an exciting road trip using Windows XP Explorer.

Microsoft Windows XP

Using Windows XP Explorer

Your organization has upgraded the operating system on each computer to Microsoft Windows XP Professional. Your supervisor has read in computer magazines that to use Windows XP effectively, people must learn Windows XP Explorer. Although almost everyone is excited about the change, those who have little experience using Windows are apprehensive about having to learn about file management. Your supervisor asks you to teach a class with an emphasis on file management to all employees who are not experienced using Windows. Your goal is to become competent using Windows XP Explorer so you can teach the class.

C A S E   P E R S P E C T I V E

Introduction

Windows XP Explorer is an application program included with Windows XP that allows you to view the contents of the computer, the hierarchy of drives and folders on the computer, and the files and folders in each folder.

Windows XP Explorer also allows you to organize the files and folders on the computer by copying and moving the files and folders. In this project, you will use Windows XP Explorer to expand and collapse drives and folders; display drive and folder contents; launch an application; select and copy a file between folders; and rename and delete a file. These are common operations that you should understand how to perform.

Launching Microsoft Windows XP

As explained in Project 1, when you turn on the computer, an introductory black screen displays for approximately one minute and then the Welcome screen displays (Figure 2-1). The Welcome screen contains a list of user icons and user names for all computer users.

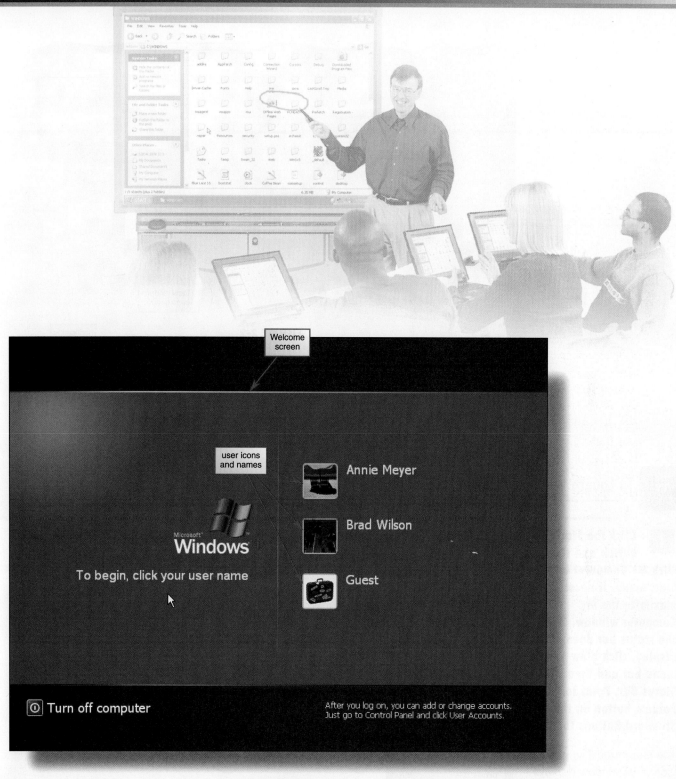

FIGURE 2-1

After launching Windows XP, you must log on to the computer by clicking your user icon on the Welcome screen, typing your password, and then clicking the Go button. As a result, the contents of the Welcome screen change, the Welcome screen displays momentarily while the log on process continues, and then the desktop displays (Figure 2-2 on the next page).

Microsoft **Windows XP**

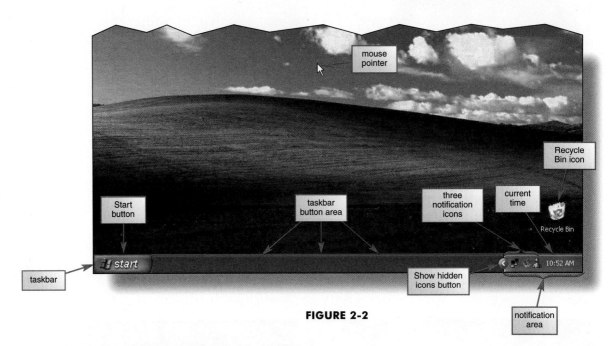

FIGURE 2-2

Launching Windows XP Explorer

As with many other operations, Windows XP offers a variety of ways to launch Windows XP Explorer. To launch Explorer using the Folders button in the My Computer window, complete the following steps.

Steps **To Launch Windows Explorer**

1 **Click the Start button and then click My Computer on the Start menu. If necessary maximize the My Computer window. If the status bar does not display, click View on the menu bar and then click Status Bar. Point to the Folders button on the Standard Buttons toolbar.**

The maximized My Computer window displays (Figure 2-3). Pointing to the Folders button on the Standard Buttons toolbar displays a three-dimensional button.

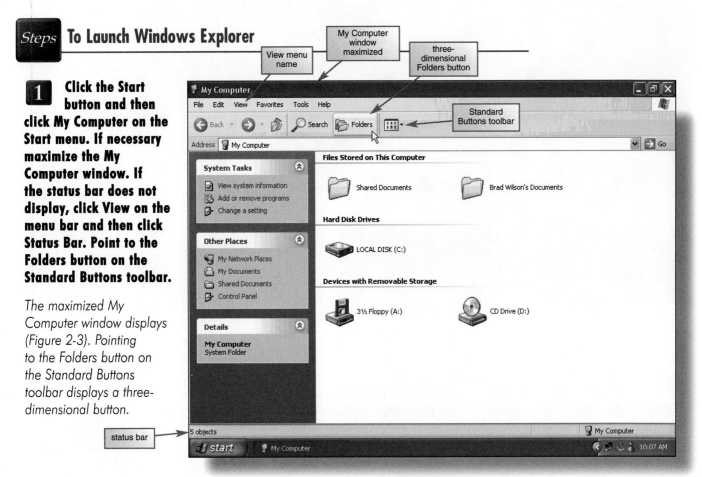

FIGURE 2-3

2 **Click the Folders button.**

The Folders pane displays in place of the left pane in the My Computer window (Figure 2-4).

FIGURE 2-4

Windows XP Explorer

When you launch Windows Explorer by clicking the Folders button in the My Computer window, the Folders button recesses and the Folders pane displays in the My Computer window (Figure 2-5).

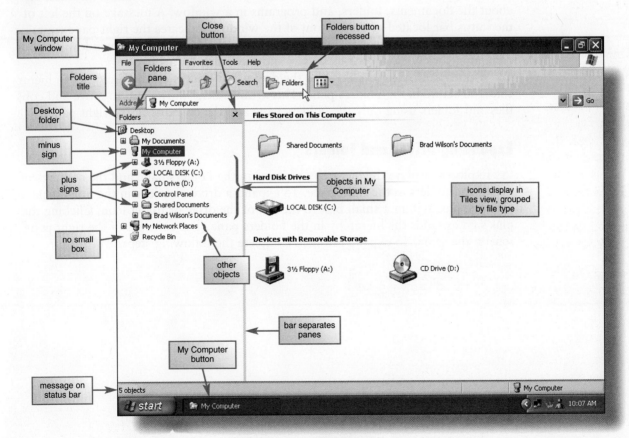

FIGURE 2-5

A Hierarchy

One definition of hierarchy in Merriam Webster's Collegiate Dictionary is a division of angels. While no one would argue angels have anything to do with Windows XP, some preach that working with a hierarchical structure is less secular (of or relating to the worldly) and more spiritual (of or relating to supernatural phenomena) than the straightforward showing of files in windows. What do you think?

The main window consists of two panes separated by a bar. The left pane of the window, called the **Folders pane** (or **Folder bar**), is identified by the Folders title and contains the hierarchical structure of files, folders, and drives on the computer. The Close button to the right of the Folders title removes the Folders pane from the My Computer window and displays the three-dimensional Folders button. A bar separates the Folders pane and the right pane of the My Computer window. You can drag the bar left or right to change the size of the Folders pane.

The top level of the hierarchy in the Folders pane is the Desktop folder. Below the Desktop folder are the My Documents, My Computer, My Network Places, and Recycle Bin icons. Your computer may have other icons.

To the left of the My Computer icon is a minus sign in a small box. The **minus sign** indicates that the drive or folder represented by the icon next to it, in this case My Computer, contains additional folders or drives and these folders or drives display below the icon. Thus, below the My Computer icon are the 3½ Floppy (A:), LOCAL DISK (C:), CD Drive (D:), Control Panel, Shared Documents, and Brad Wilson's Documents icons. Each of these icons has a small box with a plus sign next to it. The **plus sign** indicates that the drive or folder represented by the icon has more folders within it but the folders do not display in the Folders pane. As you will see, clicking the box with the plus sign will display the folders within the drive or folder represented by the icon. If an item contains no folders, such as Recycle Bin, no hierarchy exists and no small box displays next to the icon.

The right pane in the My Computer window illustrated contains three groups of icons. The Files Stored on This Computer group contains the Shared Documents icon and Brad Wilson's Documents icon. The Hard Disk Drives group contains the LOCAL DISK (C:) icon. The Devices with Removable Storage group contains the 3½ Floppy (A:) and CD Drive (D:) icons.

The **status bar** displays at the bottom of the window and contains information about the documents, folders, and programs in a window. A message on the left of the status bar located at the bottom of the window indicates the right pane contains five objects. If the status bar does not display in the My Computer window on your computer, click View on the menu bar and then click Status Bar.

Windows XP Explorer displays the drives and folders on the computer in hierarchical structure in the Folders pane. This arrangement allows you to move and copy files and folders using only the Folders pane and the contents of the right pane.

Expanding Drives and Folders

Explorer displays the hierarchy of items in the Folders pane and the contents of drives and folders in the right pane. To expand a drive or folder in the Folders pane, click the plus sign in a small box to the left of the drive or folder icon. Clicking the plus sign expands the hierarchy in the Folders pane. The contents of the right pane remain the same. To expand a folder, complete the following steps.

Steps To Expand a Folder

1 Point to the plus sign in the small box to the left of the My Documents icon in the Folders pane (Figure 2-6).

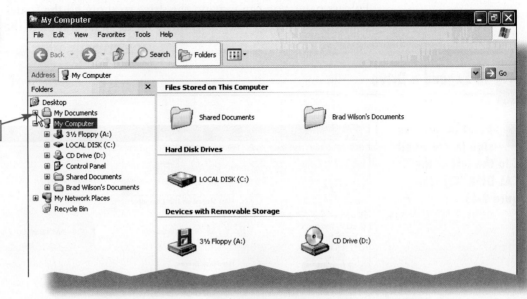

FIGURE 2-6

2 Click the plus sign.

The hierarchy below the My Documents icon expands to display the My Music folder, My Pictures folder, and My Videos folder (Figure 2-7). The minus sign to the left of the My Documents folder indicates the folder is expanded. No sign to the left of the My Music, My Pictures, and My Videos folders indicates the folders contain no additional folders. The folders in the My Documents folder on your computer may be different.

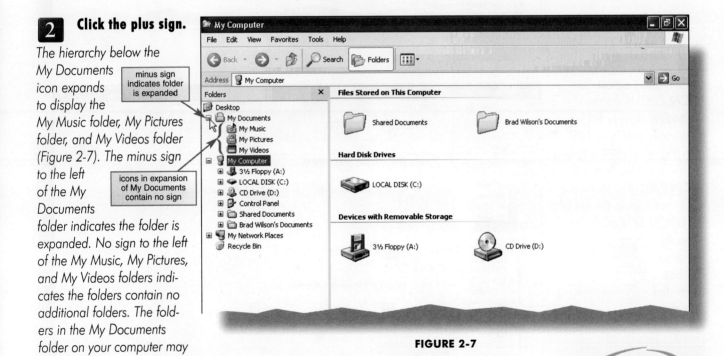

FIGURE 2-7

In Figure 2-7, the My Documents folder is expanded and the right pane still contains the contents of the My Computer folder. Clicking the plus sign next to a folder icon expands the hierarchy but does not change the contents of the right pane.

Other Ways

1. Click folder icon in Folders pane
2. Select folder to expand using ARROW keys, press PLUS on numeric keyboard
3. Select folder to expand, press RIGHT ARROW

Expanding a Drive

When a plus sign in a small box displays to the left of a drive icon in the Folders pane, you can expand the drive to show all the folders it contains. To expand drive C and view the folders on drive C, complete the following steps.

Steps **To Expand a Drive**

1 **Point to the plus sign in the small box to the left of the LOCAL DISK (C:) icon (Figure 2-8).**

FIGURE 2-8

2 **Click the plus sign.**

The hierarchy below the LOCAL DISK (C:) icon expands to display folders contained on LOCAL DISK (C:) (Figure 2-9). The folders are indented below the LOCAL DISK (C:) icon and the minus sign to the left of the LOCAL DISK (C:) icon indicates the drive has been expanded. A folder with a plus sign contains more folders.

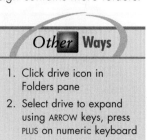

Other Ways

1. Click drive icon in Folders pane
2. Select drive to expand using ARROW keys, press PLUS on numeric keyboard
3. Select drive to expand, press RIGHT ARROW

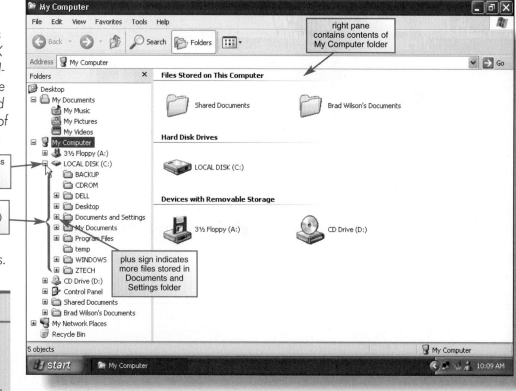

FIGURE 2-9

In Figure 2-9, the LOCAL DISK (C:) drive is expanded and the right pane still contains the contents of the My Computer folder. Clicking the plus sign next to a drive icon expands the hierarchy but does not change the contents of the right pane.

When a drive is expanded, the folders contained within the expanded drive display in the Folders pane. You can continue this expansion to view further levels of the hierarchy.

Displaying Files and Folders in Windows XP Explorer

You can display files and folders in the right pane in several different views. Currently, the files and folders in the My Computer folder display in Tiles view using Large Icons format and are grouped based upon file type. Other folders may display in a different view. The manner in which you display drive or folder contents in the right pane is a matter of personal preference.

Displaying Drive and Folder Contents

Explorer displays the hierarchy of items in the Folders pane and the contents of drives and folders in the right pane. To display the contents of a drive or folder in the right pane, click the drive or folder icon in the Folders pane. Clicking the icon displays the contents of the drive or folder in the right pane and expands the hierarchy in the Folders pane. Perform the following step to display the contents of the Shared Documents folder.

Steps **To Display the Contents of a Folder**

1 **Click the Shared Documents icon in the Folders pane.**

The selected Shared Documents name displays in the Folders pane, the hierarchy below the Shared Documents icon expands, and the right pane contains the contents of the Shared Documents folder (Figure 2-10). The window title changes to Shared Documents, the Shared Documents button replaces the My Computer button on the taskbar, and the status bar indicates two objects display in the right pane.

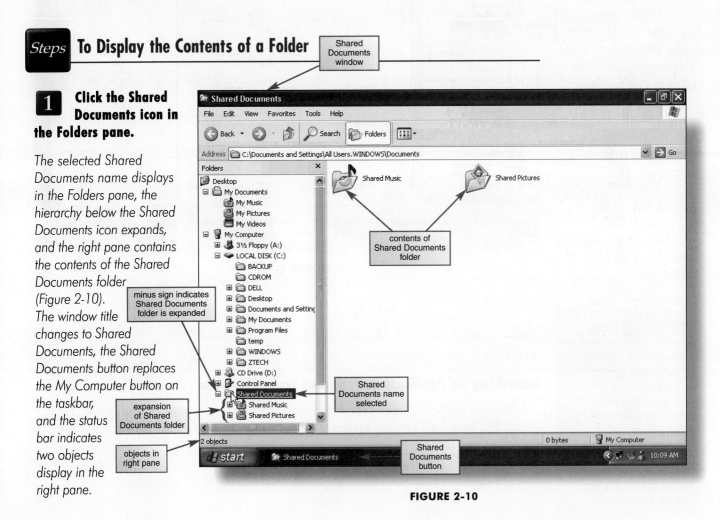

FIGURE 2-10

Whenever files or folders display in the right pane of a window, you can display the contents of a file or folder by double-clicking the icon of the file or folder.

In Figure 2-10 on the previous page, you clicked the Shared Documents icon in the Folders pane and the contents of the Shared Documents folder displayed in the right pane and the hierarchy below the Shared Documents icon expanded. If you click an icon of an expanded drive or folder, the contents of the drive or folder display in the right pane. The hierarchy below the icon will not expand because it is already expanded. To display the contents of the expanded LOCAL DISK (C:) drive, complete the following step.

Steps To Display the Contents of an Expanded Drive

1 **Click the LOCAL DISK (C:) icon in the Folders pane.**

The LOCAL DISK (C:) entry is selected in the Folders pane, the expanded Shared Documents folder collapses, and the contents of the LOCAL DISK (C:) folder display in the right pane (Figure 2-11). Notice that all the folder icons display first and then the file icons display. The status bar indicates 21 objects and 8 hidden objects occupy 328 kilobytes and the amount of space that is not being used on the disk is 10.1 gigabytes.

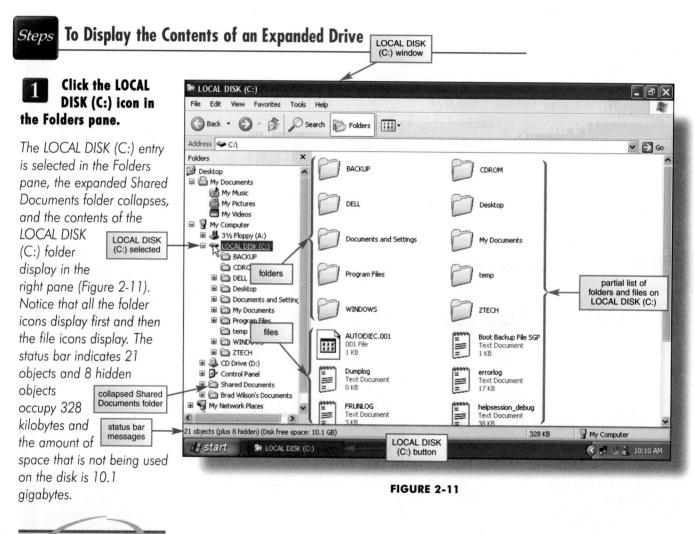

FIGURE 2-11

Other Ways

1. Double-click LOCAL DISK (C:) icon in right pane
2. Press DOWN ARROW to select LOCAL DISK (C:) icon in Folders pane
3. Press TAB to select any drive icon in right pane, press DOWN ARROW or RIGHT ARROW to select LOCAL DISK (C:) icon, press ENTER

Launching an Application Program from Explorer

You can launch an application program from the right pane of a window. To launch the Internet Explorer program stored in the Program Files folder, complete the following steps.

Steps | To Launch an Application Program from Explorer

1 Click the plus sign to the left of the Program Files icon in the Folders pane. Click the Internet Explorer icon in the Folders pane. Point to the IEXPLORE (Internet Explorer) icon in the right pane of the Internet Explorer window.

The Program Files folder and Internet Explorer folder expand, the Internet Explorer folder is selected, the window title changes to Internet Explorer, the Internet Explorer button replaces the LOCAL DISK (C:) button on the taskbar, and the contents of the Internet Explorer folder display in the right pane (Figure 2-12). The status bar indicates 6 objects and 1 hidden object consume 124 kilobytes on drive C.

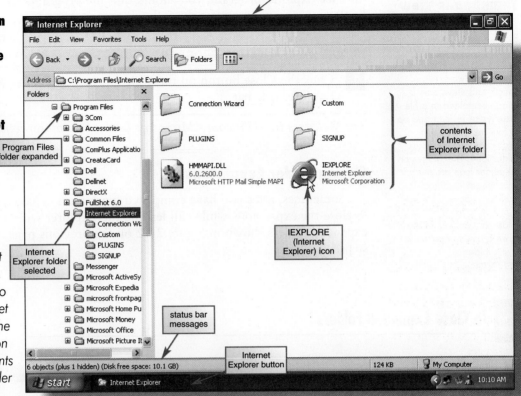

FIGURE 2-12

2 Double-click the IEXPLORE icon.

Windows XP launches the Internet Explorer program. The Welcome to MSN.com - Microsoft Internet Explorer window, containing the MSN page, displays (Figure 2-13). Because Web pages are modified frequently, the Web page that displays on your desktop may be different from the Web page shown in Figure 2-13. The URL for the Web page displays in the Address bar.

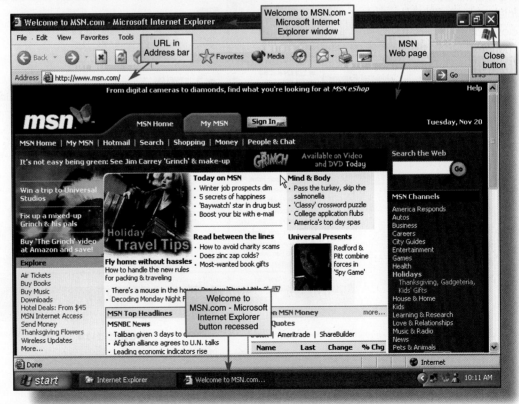

FIGURE 2-13

More About

Thumbnails View

The contents of the My Pictures window in Figure 2-17 on page WIN 2.16 displays in Thumbnails view. In Thumbnails view, the image contained in a file displays as its icon and up to four images from a folder can display on a folder icon. The images on the folder icon are the last four images modified. In addition, you can choose a picture to identify a folder that does not have to be a picture contained in the folder.

You can use the Internet Explorer program for any purpose you want, just as if you had launched it from the Start menu. When you are finished with the Internet Explorer program, you should quit the program. To quit the Internet Explorer program, complete the following step.

TO QUIT AN APPLICATION PROGRAM

1 Click the Close button on the Welcome to MSN.com - Microsoft Internet Explorer title bar.

The Welcome to MSN.com - Microsoft Internet Explorer window closes.

Closing Folder Expansions

Sometimes, after you have completed work with expanded folders, you will want to close the expansions while still leaving the Explorer window open. To close the expanded folders shown in Figure 2-12 on the previous page, complete the following steps.

Steps To Close Expanded Folders

1 Click the minus sign to the left of the Internet Explorer icon.

The expansion of the Internet Explorer folder closes and the minus sign changes to a plus sign (Figure 2-14). The contents of the right pane do not change.

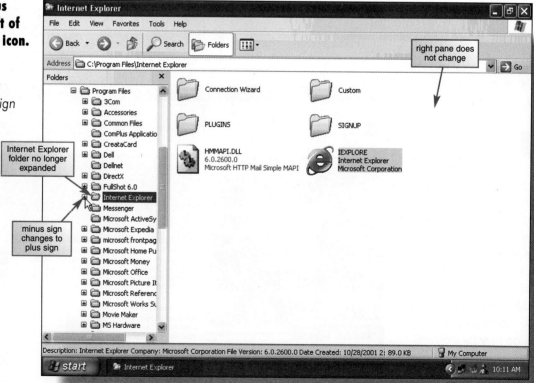

FIGURE 2-14

2 **Click the minus sign to the left of the Program Files icon.**

The expansion of the Program Files folder closes, the minus sign changes to a plus sign, the window title changes to Program Files, the Program Files button replaces the Internet Explorer button on the taskbar, and the right pane contains the files and folders in the Program Files folder (Figure 2-15).

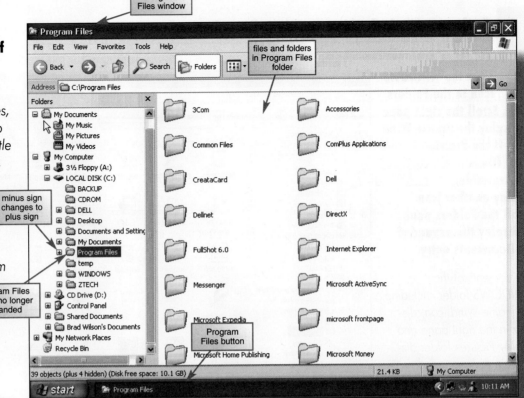

FIGURE 2-15

Moving through the Folders pane and right pane is an important skill because you will find that you use Explorer to perform a significant amount of file maintenance on the computer.

Copying, Moving, Renaming, and Deleting Files and Folders in Windows XP Explorer

You can copy, move, rename, and delete files and folders in Windows XP Explorer using essentially the same techniques as when working in folder windows. Whether you perform these activities in folder windows, in Explorer, or in a combination of the two is a personal preference. It is important for you to understand the techniques used in both cases so you can make an informed decision about how you want to perform file maintenance when using Windows XP.

Copying Files in Windows XP Explorer

In previous examples of copying files, you used the copy and paste method to copy a document file from a folder to another folder. Although you could use the copy and paste method to copy files in Windows XP Explorer, another method of copying a file is to right-drag a file (or folder) icon from the right pane to a folder or drive icon in the Folders pane. To copy the Prairie Wind file from the WINDOWS folder to the My Documents folder, complete the steps on the next page.

Other Ways

1. Click expanded folder icon, press MINUS SIGN on numeric keypad
2. Click expanded folder icon, press LEFT ARROW

Microsoft **Windows XP**

Steps **To Copy a File in Explorer by Right-Dragging**

1 Click the WINDOWS icon in the Folders pane. Scroll the right pane to display the Prairie Wind icon. If the Prairie Wind file is not available, display another icon. Scroll the Folders pane to display the expanded My Documents entry.

The contents of the WINDOWS folder, including the Prairie Wind icon, display in the right pane and the My Pictures folder displays in the expanded My Documents folder in the Folders pane (Figure 2-16).

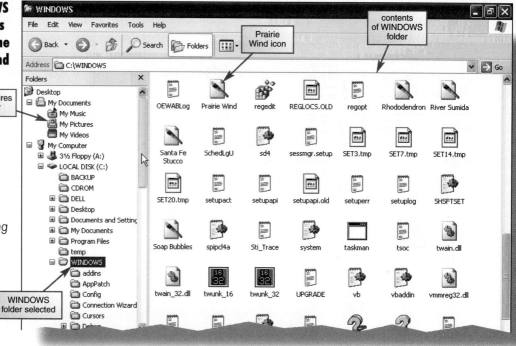

FIGURE 2-16

2 Right-drag the Prairie Wind icon onto the top of the My Pictures icon. Point to Copy Here on the shortcut menu.

The dimmed image of the Prairie Wind icon displays as you right-drag the icon onto the top of the My Pictures icon, a shortcut menu displays, and the dimmed image no longer displays (Figure 2-17).

3 Click Copy Here.

The Prairie Wind file is copied to the My Pictures folder.

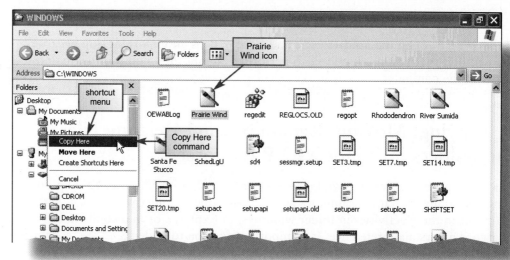

FIGURE 2-17

Other Ways

1. Right-click file to copy, click Copy, right-click My Pictures icon, click Paste

2. Click file to copy, on Edit menu click Copy, click My Pictures icon, on Edit menu click Paste

3. Select file to copy, press CTRL+C, select My Pictures icon, press CTRL+V

You can move files using the techniques just discussed except that you click **Move Here** instead of Copy Here on the shortcut menu (see Figure 2-17). The difference between a move and a copy, as mentioned previously, is that when you move a file, it is placed on the destination drive or in the destination folder and is permanently removed from its current location. When a file is copied, it is placed on the destination drive or in the destination folder as well as remaining stored in its current location.

In general, you should right-drag or use the copy and paste method to copy or move a file instead of dragging a file. If you drag a file from one folder to another on the same drive, Windows XP moves the file. If you drag a file from one folder to another folder on a different drive, Windows XP copies the file. Because of the different ways this is handled, it is strongly suggested you right-drag or use copy and paste when moving or copying files.

Displaying the Contents of the My Pictures Folder

After copying a file, you might want to examine the folder or drive where the file was copied to ensure it was copied properly. To see the contents of the My Pictures folder, complete the following step.

More About

Launching Programs in Explorer

Usually, people find starting application programs from the Start menu or from a window easier and more intuitive than starting programs from Explorer. In most cases, you will not be launching programs from Explorer.

Steps **To Display the Contents of a Folder**

1 **Click the My Pictures icon in the Folders pane.**

The contents of the My Pictures folder, including the Prairie Wind file, display in the right pane (Figure 2-18). If additional files or folders display in the My Pictures folder, their icons and titles also display.

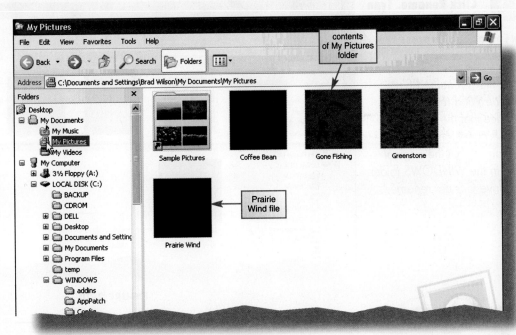

FIGURE 2-18

Renaming Files and Folders

In some circumstances, you may want to **rename** a file or a folder. This could occur when you want to distinguish a file in one folder or drive from a copy, or if you decide you need a better name to identify a file. To change the name of the Prairie Wind file in the My Pictures folder to Blue Prairie Wind, complete the steps on the next page.

Steps To Rename a File

1 **Right-click the Prairie Wind icon in the right pane and then point to Rename on the shortcut menu.**

The selected Prairie Wind icon and a shortcut menu display (Figure 2-19).

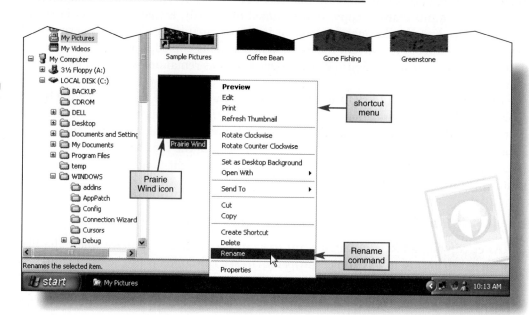

FIGURE 2-19

2 **Click Rename. Type** Blue Prairie Wind **and then press the ENTER key.**

The file is renamed Blue Prairie Wind (Figure 2-20). Notice that the file in the My Pictures folder is renamed, but the original file in the WINDOWS folder in drive C is not renamed.

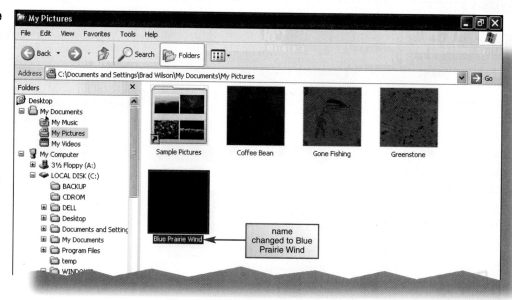

FIGURE 2-20

1. Right-click icon, press M, type name, press ENTER

2. Click icon, press F2, type name, press ENTER

3. Click icon, on File menu click Rename, type name, press ENTER

4. Select icon, press ALT+F, press M, type name, press ENTER

Renaming files by the method shown above also can be accomplished in other windows. For example, if you open the My Computer window and then open the My Music window, you can rename any file stored in the My Music window using the technique just presented.

Use caution when renaming files on the hard disk. If you inadvertently rename a file that is associated with certain programs, the programs may not be able to find the file and, therefore, may not execute properly.

If you change a file name for which a shortcut exists on a menu, in a folder, or on the desktop, Windows XP will update the shortcut link so the shortcut points to the renamed file. The name of the shortcut, however, does not change to reflect the name change of the linked file.

Deleting Files in Windows XP Explorer

A final function that you may want to use in Windows XP Explorer is to delete a file. Exercise extreme caution when deleting a file or files. When you delete a file from a floppy disk, the file is gone permanently once you delete it. If you delete a file from a hard disk, the deleted file is stored in the Recycle Bin where you can recover it until you empty the Recycle Bin.

Assume you have decided to delete the Greenstone file from the My Pictures window. To delete the Greenstone file, complete the following steps.

More About

Deleting Files

This is your last warning! Be EXTREMELY careful when deleting files. Hours of work can be lost with one click of a button. If you are going to delete files or folders from your hard disk, make a backup of those files to ensure that if you inadvertently delete something you need, you will be able to recover the file.

Steps **To Delete a File by Right-Dragging to the Recycle Bin**

1 **Scroll the Folders pane to display the Recycle Bin icon. Right-drag the Greenstone icon to the Recycle Bin icon in the Folders pane and then point to Move Here on the shortcut menu.**

The Greenstone icon in the right pane is right-dragged to the Recycle Bin icon in the Folders pane and a shortcut menu displays (Figure 2-21). The Move Here command is highlighted on the shortcut menu.

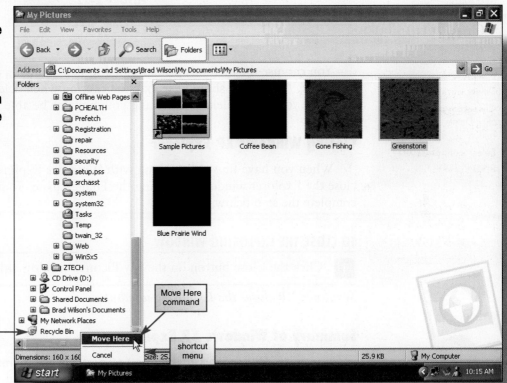

FIGURE 2-21

2 **Click Move Here.**

The Greenstone icon is removed from the right pane and moved to the Recycle Bin (Figure 2-22). The icons in the right pane are rearranged and the Blue Prairie Wind icon displays in the location the Greenstone icon occupied before being deleted. If you wish to terminate the deleting process before it is complete, you can click the Cancel button on the shortcut menu.

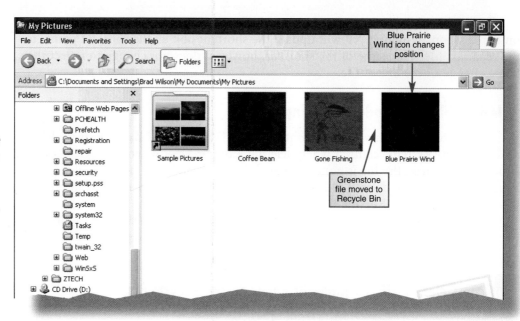

FIGURE 2-22

1. Drag icon to Recycle Bin
2. Right-click icon, click Delete, click Yes button
3. Click icon, on File menu click Delete, click Yes button
4. Select icon, press ALT+F, press D, press Y

You can use the methods just specified to delete folders on a floppy disk or a hard disk. Again, you should use extreme caution when deleting files and folders to ensure you do not delete something you may not be able to recover.

Closing Windows XP Explorer

When you have finished working with Windows Explorer, normally you will close the Explorer window by closing the Folders pane. To close the Folders pane, complete the step below.

TO CLOSE THE EXPLORING WINDOW

1 Click the Close button on the My Pictures window title bar.

Windows XP closes the Exploring window.

Summary of Windows XP Explorer

Windows XP Explorer enables you to perform file maintenance in a single window without displaying additional windows or worrying about window management on the desktop. In addition, it provides a hierarchical view of all drives, folders, and files on the computer. Whether you choose to use Explorer or the My Computer window to perform file maintenance is a personal choice. You may find that some tasks are easier using Explorer and others are easier using the My Computer window.

Logging Off and Turning Off the Computer

After completing your work with Windows XP, you should close your user account by logging off from the computer. Perform the following steps to log off from the computer.

TO LOG OFF FROM THE COMPUTER

1 Click the Start button on the taskbar.

2 Click Log Off on the Start menu.

3 Click the Log Off button in the Log Off Windows dialog box.

Windows XP logs off from the computer and displays the Welcome screen.

After logging off, you also may want to turn off the computer. If you are sure you want to turn off the computer, perform the following steps. If you are not sure about turning off the computer, read the following steps without actually performing them.

TO TURN OFF THE COMPUTER

1 Click the Turn off computer link on the Welcome screen.

2 Click the Turn Off button in the Turn off computer dialog box.

Windows XP is shut down.

CASE PERSPECTIVE SUMMARY

Your supervisor emphasizes the importance of computer users being able to use Windows XP Explorer effectively to control and manage files and folders on their computers. With this in mind, you developed a one-hour class for employees with little computer experience and offered the classes during normal business hours, on alternating weeknights, and on Saturday mornings. Your supervisor was pleased with the results and recommended you for a newly-developed position in his department.

Project Summary

In this project, you launched Windows XP Explorer, expanded drives and folders, displayed the contents of files and folders, launched an application program from Explorer, closed drive and folder expansions, copied and renamed files, deleted files, and closed Windows XP.

What You Should Know

Having completed this project, you now should be able to perform the following tasks:

▶ Close Expanded Folders *(WIN 2.14)*
▶ Close the Exploring Window *(WIN 2.20)*
▶ Copy a File in Explorer by Right-Dragging *(WIN 2.16)*
▶ Delete a File by Right-Dragging to the Recycle Bin *(WIN 2.19)*
▶ Display the Contents of a Folder *(WIN 2.11, WIN 2.17)*
▶ Display the Contents of an Expanded Drive *(WIN 2.12)*

▶ Expand a Drive *(WIN 2.10)*
▶ Expand a Folder *(WIN 2.09)*
▶ Launch an Application Program from Explorer *(WIN 2.13)*
▶ Launch Windows Explorer *(WIN 2.06)*
▶ Log Off from the Computer *(WIN 2.21)*
▶ Quit an Application Program *(WIN 2.14)*
▶ Rename a File *(WIN 2.18)*
▶ Turn Off the Computer *(WIN 2.21)*

Learn It Online

Instructions: To complete the Learn It Online exercises, launch your Web browser using the steps on page WIN 1.41, click the Address box, enter scsite.com/winxp/exs.htm, and then press the ENTER key. When the Windows XP Learn It Online page displays, follow the instructions in the exercises below.

1 Project Reinforcement TF, MC, and SA

Below Windows XP Project 2, click the Project Reinforcement link. Print the quiz by clicking Print on the File menu. Answer each question. Write your first and last name at the top of each page, and then hand in the printout to your instructor.

2 Flash Cards

Below Windows XP Project 2, click the Flash Cards link. When Flash Cards displays, read the instructions. Type 20 (or a number specified by your instructor) in the Number of Playing Cards text box, type your name in the Name text box, and then click the Flip Card button. When the flash card displays, read the question and then click the Answer box arrow to select an answer. Flip through Flash Cards. Click Print on the File menu to print the last flash card if your score is 15 (75%) correct or greater and then hand it in to your instructor. If your score is less than 15 (75%) correct, then redo this exercise by clicking the Replay button.

3 Practice Test

Below Windows XP Project 2, click the Practice Test link. Answer each question, enter your first and last name at the bottom of the page, and then click the Grade Test button. When the graded practice test displays on your screen, click Print on the File menu to print a hard copy. Continue to take practice tests until you score 80% or better. Hand in a printout of the final practice test to your instructor.

4 Who Wants to Be a Computer Genius?

Below Windows XP Project 2, click the Computer Genius link. Read the instructions, enter your first and last name at the bottom of the page, and then click the Play button. Hand in a printout of your score to your instructor.

5 Wheel of Terms

Below Windows XP Project 2, click the Wheel of Terms link. Read the instructions, and then enter your first and last name and your school name. Click the Play button. Hand in a printout of your score to your instructor.

6 Crossword Puzzle Challenge

Below Windows XP Project 2, click the Crossword Puzzle Challenge link. Read the instructions, and then enter your first and last name. Click the Play button. Work the crossword puzzle. When you are finished, click the Submit button. When the crossword puzzle redisplays, click the Print button. Hand in the printout.

7 Tips and Tricks

Below Windows XP Project 2, click the Tips and Tricks link. Click a topic that pertains to Project 2. Right-click the information and then click Print on the shortcut menu. Construct a brief example of what the information relates to in Windows XP to confirm that you understand how to use the tip or trick. Hand in the example and printed information.

o n l i n e

8 Newsgroups

Below Windows XP Project 2, click the Newsgroups link. Click a topic that pertains to Project 2. Print three comments. Hand in the comments to your instructor.

9 Expanding Your Horizons

Below Windows XP Project 2, click the Expanding Your Horizons link. Click a topic that pertains to Project 2. Print the information. Construct a brief example of what the information relates to in Windows XP to confirm that you understand the contents of the article. Hand in the example and printed information to your instructor.

10 Search Sleuth

Below Windows XP Project 2, click the Search Sleuth link. To search for a term that pertains to this project, select a term below the Project 2 title and then use the Google search engine at google.com (or any major search engine) to display and print two Web pages that present information on the term. Hand in the printouts to your instructor.

Use Help

1 Using Windows Help and Support

Instructions: Use Windows Help and Support to perform the following tasks.

1. If necessary, launch Microsoft Windows XP and log on to the computer.

2. Launch Windows Help and Support. In the Help and Support Center window, click the Index button, and then type `windows explorer` in the Type in the keyword to find text box. Answer the following questions about Windows Explorer.

    a. What method is recommended for copying a file or folder?
    _____

    b. What dialog box can be used to add the My Documents icon to the desktop?
    _____
    _____

    c. What keyboard shortcuts are used to perform the following tasks?
    Copy a file _____   Paste a file _____
    Rename a file _____   Search for a file _____
    Collapse a folder in Explorer _____

3. You recently wrote a business letter to a friend explaining how to install Microsoft Windows XP Professional. You want to see what else you said in the letter, but you cannot remember the name of the file or where you stored the file on the computer. You decide to check Windows Help and Support to determine the locations you could check to find a lost file. List the first two locations suggested by Windows Help and Support. Write those locations in the spaces provided.
    Location 1: _____
    Location 2: _____

4. You and your brother each have a computer in your bedroom. A printer is attached to your computer. Your brother, whose computer does not have a printer, would like to print some of his more colorful images using the printer attached to your computer. You have heard that for a reasonable cost you can create a home network to connect the two computers. Then, your brother can print documents stored on his computer on the printer connected to your computer. Using Windows Help and Support, determine what equipment is needed to connect two computers in an Ethernet network. Print the Help pages that document your answer.

5. The Windows XP Professional operating system is installed on your computer and the computer is connected to a network. You read in a computer magazine that Windows XP has tools designed for working with files stored on your computer and files stored on the network. You are unsure whether you should use My Briefcase or Offline Files to work with the files on your computer. Using Windows Help, learn about the difference between My Briefcase and Offline Files. Print the Help pages that explain My Briefcase and Offline Files.

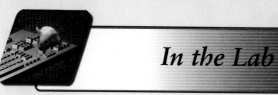

In the Lab

1 Launching Windows Explorer

Instructions: Use a computer to perform the following tasks and answer the questions.

Part 1: *Launching Explorer with the Folders Button*

1. If necessary, launch Microsoft Windows XP and log on to the computer.
2. Click the Start button and then click My Computer on the Start menu.
3. Click the Folders button in the My Computer window. Answer the following questions.
   a. Which folder is highlighted in the Folders pane? _____
   b. Which folders are contained in the highlighted folder? _____
   _____
   c. Which icons are preceded by a minus sign? _____
4. Click the Close button in the My Computer window.

Part 2: *Launching Explorer Using the Computer Command*

1. Click the Start button and then right-click My Computer on the Start menu.
2. Click Explore on the shortcut menu. Answer the following questions.
   a. Which folder is highlighted in the Folders pane? _____
   b. Which folders are contained in the highlighted folder? _____
   _____
   c. Which icons are preceded by a minus sign? _____
   d. How do the answers in a, b, and c compare to the answers in Part 1, Step 3 above?
   _____
3. Click the Close button in the My Computer window.

Part 3: *Launching Explorer by Right-Clicking the Start Button*

1. Right-click the Start button and then click Explore on the shortcut menu. Answer the following questions.
   a. Which folder is highlighted in the Folders pane? _____
   b. Which folders are contained in the highlighted folder? _____
   _____
   c. Which icons are preceded by a minus sign? _____
   _____
2. Click the Close button in the window.

Part 4: *Launching Explorer by Right-Clicking a Desktop Icon*

1. Right-click the Recycle Bin button and then click Explore on the shortcut menu. Answer the following questions.
   a. Which folder is highlighted in the Folders pane? _____
   b. Which folders are contained in the highlighted folder? _____
   c. Which icons are preceded by a minus sign? _____
2. Click the Close button in the Recycle Bin window.

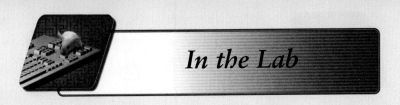

In the Lab

Part 5: *Launching Explorer by Right-Clicking a Start Menu Command*

1. Click the Start button and then right-click My Pictures on the Start menu.
2. Click Explore on the shortcut menu. Answer the following questions.
   a. Which folder is highlighted in the Folders pane? _____
   b. Which folders are contained in the highlighted folder? _____
   _____
   c. Which icons are preceded by a minus sign? _____
3. Click the Close button in the window.

2 File, Folder, and Program Properties

Instructions: Use a computer to perform the following tasks and answer the questions.

Part 1: *Displaying File Properties*

1. If necessary, launch Microsoft Windows XP and log on to the computer.
2. Click the Start button and then click My Computer on the Start menu.
3. Click the Folders button in the My Computer window.
4. Double-click the LOCAL DISK (C:) icon. If necessary, click Show the contents of this folder.
5. Double-click the WINDOWS icon. If necessary, click the Show the contents of this folder link.
6. Scroll the right pane until the Soap Bubbles icon is visible. If the Soap Bubbles icon is not available on your computer, find the icon of another file.
7. Right-click the Soap Bubbles icon. Click Properties on the shortcut menu. Answer the following questions about the Soap Bubbles file:
   a. What type of file is Soap Bubbles? _____
   b. What program is used to open the Soap Bubbles image? _____
   c. What is the path (location) of the Soap Bubbles file? _____
   d. What is the size (in bytes) of the Soap Bubbles file? _____
   e. When was the file created? _____
   f. When was the file last modified? _____
   g. When was the file last accessed? _____
8. Click the Close button in the Soap Bubbles Properties dialog box.

Part 2: *Displaying Program Properties*

1. Scroll the right pane of the WINDOWS window until the notepad icon displays.
2. Right-click the notepad icon. Click Properties on the shortcut menu. Answer the following questions.
   a. What type of file is notepad? _____
   b. What is the file's description? _____
   c. What is the path (location) of the notepad file? _____
   d. What size is the notepad file when stored on disk? _____
3. Click the Close button in the notepad Properties dialog box.

(continued)

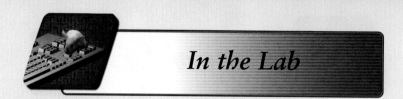

In the Lab

File, Folder, and Program Properties *(continued)*

Part 3: *Displaying Folder Properties*

1. Scroll the right pane of the WINDOWS window until the Help icon displays.
2. Right-click the Help icon. Click Properties on the shortcut menu. Answer the following questions.
   a. What type of folder is Help? _____
   b. What is the path (location) of the Help folder? _____
   c. How many files are stored in the Help folder? _____
   d. How many folders are stored in the Help folder? _____
3. Click the Close button in the Help Properties dialog box.
4. Close the WINDOWS window.

3 Windows Explorer

Instructions: Use a computer to perform the following tasks and answer the questions.

Part 1: *Launching the Internet Explorer Program*

1. If necessary, launch Microsoft Windows XP and log on to the computer.
2. Click the Start button and then click My Computer on the Start menu.
3. Click the Folders button on the Standard Buttons toolbar.
4. Expand the LOCAL DISK (C:) folder.
5. Expand the Program Files folder.
6. Display the contents of the Internet Explorer folder.
7. Double-click the IEXPLORE icon to launch Internet Explorer and display the Microsoft Internet Explorer window.

Part 2: *Finding and Saving Logo Images*

1. Type www.jellybelly.com in the Address bar in the Microsoft Internet Explorer window and click the Go button.
2. Find the jelly belly logo, right-click the jelly belly logo, click Save Picture As on the shortcut menu, type Jelly Belly logo in the File name box in the Save Picture dialog box, and then click the Save button to save the logo in the My Pictures folder.
3. Repeat Steps 1 and 2 above but type www.snapple.com and use the file name, Snapple logo, to save the Snapple logo in the My Pictures folder.
4. Repeat Steps 1 and 2 above but type www.gatorade.com and use the file name, Gatorade logo, to save the Gatorade logo in the My Pictures folder.
5. Repeat Steps 1 and 2 above but type www.jollyrancherfruitchews.com and use the file name, Jolly Rancher logo, to save the Jolly Rancher logo in the My Pictures folder.
6. The Jelly Belly logo, Snapple logo, Gatorade logo, and Jolly Rancher logo display in the My Pictures window (Figure 2-23). The logos in the My Pictures window on your computer may be different from the logos shown in Figure 2-23 because businesses may change their logos.

In the Lab

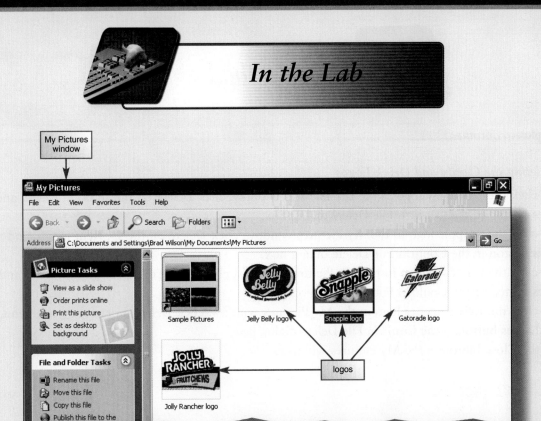

FIGURE 2-23

7. Click the Close button in the Jolly Rancher Fruit Chews - Microsoft Internet Explorer window.
8. Click the Close button in the Internet Explorer window.

Part 3: *Displaying File Properties*

1. Click the Start button and then click My Pictures on the Start menu.
2. Right-click each logo file in the My Pictures window, click Properties, answer the question about the logo below, and then close the Properties dialog box.
   a. What type of file is the Jelly Belly logo file? _____
   b. What type of file is the Snapple logo file? _____
   c. What type of file is the Gatorade logo file? _____
   d. What type of file is the Jolly Rancher logo file? _____
3. Click an open area of the My Pictures window to deselect the Jolly Rogers logo file.

Part 4: *Printing the Logo Images*

1. Click Print pictures in the Picture Tasks area in the My Pictures window to start the Photo Printing Wizard.
2. Click the Next button in the Photo Printing Wizard window.
3. Verify a check mark displays in the upper-right corner of each logo. Click the Next button.
4. Verify the correct printer is being used. Click the Next button.
5. Scroll the Available layouts box to display the 3.5 x 5 in. Prints area. Click the image in the area to select the image. Click the Next button to print the images.
6. Click the Finish button in the Photo Printing Wizard window.

(continued)

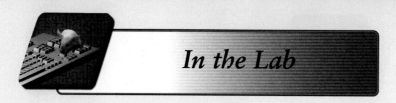

In the Lab

Windows Explorer *(continued)*

Part 5: *Deleting the Candy and Drink Logos*

1. Right-click the Jelly Belly logo in the My Pictures window, click Delete on the shortcut menu, and then click the Yes button in the Confirm File Delete dialog box.
2. Right-click the Snapple logo in the My Pictures window, click Delete on the shortcut menu, and then click the Yes button in the Confirm File Delete dialog box.
3. Right-click the Gatorade logo in the My Pictures window, click Delete on the shortcut menu, and then click the Yes button in the Confirm File Delete dialog box.
4. Right-click the Jolly Rancher logo in the My Pictures window, click Delete on the shortcut menu, and then click the Yes button in the Confirm File Delete dialog box.
5. Click the Close button in the My Pictures window.

Cases and Places

The difficulty of these case studies varies:
▶ are the least difficult; ▶▶ are more difficult; and ▶▶▶ are the most difficult.

1 ▶ An interesting feature of Windows XP is the capability of changing the format of the icons in the right pane of a window. Using Windows Explorer, display the contents of the Local Disk (C:) folder and then experiment with the five commands on the View menu. Describe the effects of the Thumbnails, Tiles, Icons, List, and Details commands on the icons in the right pane. When using Details view, explain how clicking one of the buttons at the top of the right pane (such as Name or Size) changes the window. Finally, specify situations in which you think some of the views you have seen would be most appropriate.

2 ▶ Backing up files is an important way to protect data and ensure it is not lost or destroyed accidentally. File backup on a personal computer can use a variety of devices and techniques. Using the Internet, a library, personal computer magazines, and other resources, determine the types of devices used to store backed up data, schedules, methods, and techniques for backing up data, and the consequences of not backing up data. Write a brief report of your findings.

3 ▶▶ A hard disk must be maintained to be used most efficiently. This maintenance includes deleting old files, defragmenting a disk so it does not waste space, and from time to time, finding and attempting to correct disk failures. Using the Internet, a library, Windows XP Help and Support, and other research facilities, determine the maintenance that should be performed on hard disks. This includes the type of maintenance, when it should be performed, how long it takes to perform the maintenance, and the risks of not performing the maintenance. Write a brief report on the information you obtain.

4 ▶▶ A file system is the overall structure in which files are named, stored, and organized. Windows XP supports three file systems: FAT, FAT32, and NTFS. You must choose a file system when you install Windows XP, install a new hard disk, or format an existing hard disk or floppy disk. Before deciding which file system is right for you, you should research the three file systems to understand the benefits and limitations of each system. Write a brief report comparing the three file systems. Discuss the benefits and limitations of each system.

5 ▶▶▶ Data stored on disk is one of a company's most valuable assets. If that data were to be stolen, lost, or compromised so it could not be accessed, the company could go out of business. Therefore, companies go to great lengths to protect their data. Visit a company or business in your area. Find out how it protects its data against viruses, unauthorized access, and even against such natural disasters as fire and floods. Prepare a brief report that describes the company's procedures. In your report, point out any areas where you find the company has not protected its data adequately.

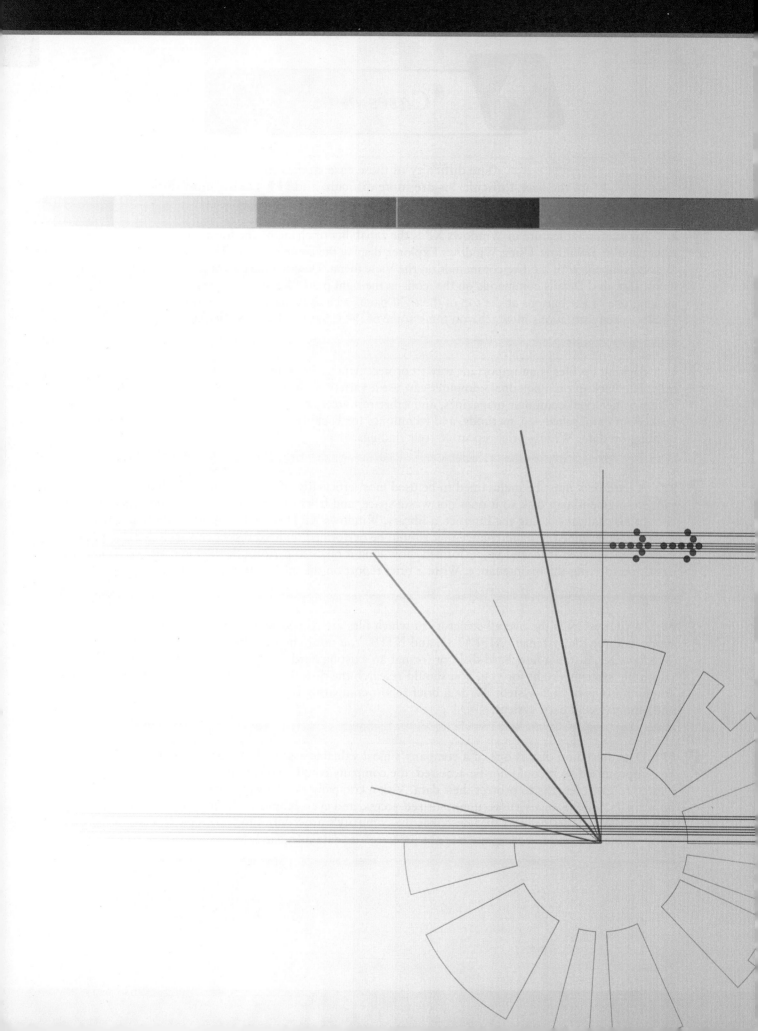

APPENDIX A

New Features of Windows XP Professional and Windows XP Home Edition

Microsoft Windows XP delivers a high standard in reliability and performance. Its many new features make it easier to use than previous versions of Windows. Windows XP is available in two editions: Microsoft Windows XP Professional and Microsoft Windows XP Home Edition. Windows XP Professional is designed for business and power users and includes advanced features for high-level performance and fast system response time. Windows XP Home Edition is intended for home computing and offers many new features that help home users work efficiently and connect faster to the Internet and with others. Table A-1 provides a list of the new features in Windows XP. The left column summarizes the major features of Windows XP Professional. The right column indicates whether the feature is available in Windows XP Home Edition.

Table A-1 Windows XP New Features and Comparison of Professional and Home Edition

WINDOWS XP PROFESSIONAL NEW FEATURES	AVAILABLE IN WINDOWS XP HOME EDITION
Access to all your documents and settings no matter which computer you use to log on	No
Access to files and folders on a network share when disconnected from the server	No
Advanced notebook support, including ClearType support, Dualview, and power management improvements	Yes
Allows multiple applications to run simultaneously	Yes
Automated System Recovery (ASR) assists in recovering from a major system error	No
Automatic 802.1x wireless network configuration	Yes
Automatically install, configure, repair, or remove software applications	No
CD burning lets you create CDs by dragging in Windows Explorer	Yes
Encrypting File System (EFS) allows encrypting of individual files or folders for security of files and folders on a local computer (not a network computer)	No
Faster boot and resume times	Yes
File-level access control allows an administrator with administrative privileges to limit access to some network resources (servers, directories, and files)	No
Help and Support Center lets you access Microsoft Knowledge Base on the Internet and access frequently used Help topics	Yes
Home networking	Yes
Internet Connection Firewall	Yes
Internet Information Services/Personal Web Server - IIS Web Server 5.1	No

(continued)

Table A-1   Windows XP New Features and Comparison of Professional and Home Edition *(continued)*

WINDOWS XP PROFESSIONAL NEW FEATURES	AVAILABLE IN WINDOWS XP HOME EDITION
Maintain control over personal information when visiting Web sites	Yes
Multi-lingual User Interface (MUI) add-on	No
Multi-processor support of up to two microprocessors	No
My Pictures and My Music folders let you organize and manipulate pictures and music	Yes
Network Setup Wizard	Yes
New user interface	Yes
Opened files grouped under one taskbar button making it easier to work with many files at the same time	Yes
Powerful management and security tools	No
Remote Desktop allows control of an office computer from home as though you are sitting in front of the office computer	No
Remote Installation Service	No
Restrict access to selected files, applications, and other resources	No
Scalable processor support	No
Scanner and Camera Wizard steps you through scanning images	Yes
Search Companion identifies the kind of help needed and retrieves relevant information	Yes
Simplifies procedures for administration of groups of users or computers	No
Single Worldwide Binary	Yes
Start menu organizes programs and frequently used tasks	Yes
System restore lets you restore computer to a previous version	Yes
Use of task panes containing commands and options in My Computer and My Documents windows	Yes
Welcome screen lets you share the same computer with others	Yes
Windows Media Player allows you to work with digital media files, watch DVD movies, and listen to radio stations	Yes
Windows Messenger lets you communicate with others	Yes

Index